Human
Justice

D1738249

Human Justice

Human and the Lights

gatekeeper press™
Tampa, Florida

Human Justice

Published by Gatekeeper Press
7853 Gunn Hwy., Suite 209
Tampa, FL 33626
www.GatekeeperPress.com

Library of Congress Control Number: 2023951857

ISBN (paperback): 9781662947162
eISBN: 9781662947179

To the best of my judgment,
when I look at the human character,
I see no virtue placed there
to counter justice.

....

MARCUS AURELIUS

CONTENTS

PROLOGUE

During bad circumstances, which is the
human inheritance, you must decide not to be reduced.
You have your humanity, and you must not
allow anything to reduce that.

....

MAYA ANGELOU

Human Values

~2017, 8 a.m.

Just ended a phone call with my client, Karen.* She accused her boss of firing her because she told him she had epilepsy.

Karen said the document she e-faxed me minutes ago was a doctor's note confirming the epilepsy diagnosis.

I believe the thing to be a forgery and Karen to be a liar.

A paid settlement conference in Karen's wrongful termination lawsuit starts in one hour.

———————

* I changed names, timelines, and a few details in this booklet, but I otherwise did my best to be honest and accurate.

1

The human value of honesty should compel me to withdraw as her lawyer.

Instead, I settle her case for about a year's lost wages. I take 40 percent plus $4,000 in advanced litigation costs out of Karen's recovery as attorney fees and expenses.

I'm only Human.

Corporate Values

Abundance is not something we acquire.
It is something we tune into.

....
WAYNE DYER

I was a human rights lawyer for 15 years. I helped humans enforce civil rights and anti-discrimination laws. Most of my clients were financially poor humans descended from slaves.

Fighting for poor folks harmed by corporate iniquity opened my eyes to a grim reality: We live in an age controlled by and for corporations.

Someone said these kinds of cases are always about human values versus corporate values.

Corporate values are always amoral. The sole criterion of corporate decision-making is maximizing profit. That's it. There's no consideration of human values. Nothing about:
- Spirituality
- Humility

- Compassion
- Kindness
- Integrity
- Selflessness
- Empathy
- Love

Only money.

The harmonic divide reverberating in society is less about blue values versus red values and more about human values versus corporate values.

The corporates are winning.

And as Karen's story demonstrates, even the most well-meaning among us are helping the corporate side win when we choose to accept their values and play by their rules. This needs to stop.

Human values must always trump corporate values.

INTRODUCTION

Never whisper justice.

....

ALAN PAGE

After Karen's case, I tried to quit lawyering. Failing at that, I tried something new and, as it turns out, revolutionary. I started treating potential new clients like humans.

Treating potential clients like humans changed the game. I became more selective. I didn't offer to represent someone unless they said they would go to trial and testify under oath if necessary.

Most of my white clients' cases settled for amounts about equal to their economic losses, such as lost wages.

In most of my non-white clients' cases, the other side offered nothing or close to it. We had to settle for nuisance value or go to trial.

I advised all my clients to refuse to settle for cheap justice and instead go to trial.

Money is the only form of justice available under the civil justice system. I requested juries to allow my clients to recover money for their economic losses. Most juries complied. Then I asked juries to allow my clients to recover money for their spiritual harms. Most juries complied with that request, too.

Six years after Karen's case, I had the honor of representing Mr. Theodore Brown in my last trial before leaving the law to focus on leading with my heart.

Corporate values played out to their logical extreme in Mr. Brown's case. What happened signaled that the corporatism dominating our society is incompatible with a sustainable future for our species and our planet.

This is the true story of what happened.

∞

The text below is a lightly edited draft of the opening statement I made at Mr. Brown's trial.

TED BROWN – OPENING STATEMENT

Good morning.

I. BIG RULES OF THE ROAD

Employers may not discriminate or retaliate against workers who suffer work injuries or report discrimination.

If an employer discriminates or retaliates against a worker who suffered a work injury or reported discrimination, the employer did not follow the rules and is responsible for all resulting harm.

II. THE STORY OF WHAT DEFENDANT DID

Let me tell you the story of what happened in this case.

Let's go back to spring 2020. Good Paper Company's corporate offices.

Good Paper Company is a wholesale distributor of paper and packaging products that operated Monday through Friday, 24 hours a day and is closed on weekends for cleaning.

In the spring of 2020, Good Paper leadership receives a report about unsafe work conditions from a warehouse employee, a 61-year-old Black man with decades of experience working in warehouse settings.

Good Paper leadership learns the employee reported to his supervisor that there were trailer truck doors in the warehouse that were off track and falling down on their own, and that he was concerned someone might get hurt.

A couple of weeks later, Good Paper leadership learns that the employee made a second safety complaint, this time to the third shift manager, that the trailer truck doors in the warehouse had not been fixed and kept falling down.

A couple of weeks after the second complaint, Good Paper leadership learns that the employee made a third safety complaint about the broken trailer doors, this time to the second shift manager.

A couple of months after the employee's first complaint about the broken trailer truck door, Good Paper leadership learns that the heavy door fell open and hit the employee, badly injuring his neck, back, and head.

Good Paper leadership learns that the injured employee had to leave work and go to the emergency room twice in two days to treat his injuries, and that his health care providers prescribed him a narcotic medication and took him off work for an extended period of time.

Introduction

Good Paper leadership learns that the injured employee brought a workers' compensation claim in connection with his work injuries.

Good Paper leadership receives complaints from the injured employee that its HR Manager called him repeatedly while he was on leave to pressure him to quit his job, which would have cut off his ability to receive workers' compensation benefits.

About a month after the door fell on the injured employee, Good Paper leadership learns that he had returned to work and that his health care providers gave him a 20-pound lifting restriction.

Good Paper leadership receives reports from the injured employee complaining about his supervisors assigning him tasks that exceed his lifting restrictions, which worsened his pain and injuries and caused him to miss more work.

Good Paper leadership receives reports from the employee that his supervisors were harassing him for having work restrictions, including calling him the N-word.

Good Paper leadership tells the injured employee that the harassment is his fault because his work restrictions forced other workers to work longer hours.

Good Paper leadership receives a report from the employee that he missed work due to his work injuries flaring up after a supervisor made him lift 120 boxes in a row that each weighed at or near the upper limits of his work restrictions.

Good Paper learns from the employee that the employee believed his supervisor made him lift the boxes as harassment and retaliation for his work injuries and restrictions.

Good Paper leadership learns that at the beginning of the employee's next shift after the box-lifting punishment, the employee told his supervisor that he needed to miss work due to the pain, called in to work according to Good Paper's procedures the next day, and obtained a doctor's note excusing him for his work absences.

Good Paper terminates the injured employee for missing three shifts due to his work injuries, even though the warehouse was closed on the days it said it fired the injured employee for missing.

Good Paper leadership learns that its reason for termination is false, as the shifts it said it terminated the injured employee for missing did not exist.

Good Paper leadership allows the termination decision to stand.

Good Paper sells the company to another corporate entity, Best Paper, LLC, and changes its name to Best Paper.

Good Paper and whoever else makes the decisions for a company that no longer exists sue the injured employee in district court for asserting his civil rights.

The employee is Mr. Theodore Brown. You met him earlier today.

There is no dispute that Good Paper and its lawyers admit that they fired Mr. Brown for missing shifts on days when the plant was not even open.

There is no dispute that Good Paper's reason for firing Mr. Brown lacks any basis in fact.

The evidence will show it is more likely than not that discrimination and retaliation motivated the decision to terminate Mr. Brown's employment.

III. WHO WE ARE SUING AND WHY

Let me tell you who we are suing and why.

We are suing Good Paper Company and Best Paper, LLC, for two reasons.

A. RULE-VIOLATING ACT

The first reason is that Good Paper Company fired a worker out of discrimination because of his disabling work injury, and in retaliation because he reported discrimination.

Good Paper Company and its lawyers confirmed in writing that Good Paper's stated reason for terminating Mr. Brown is false.

Good Paper's lies show that it is more likely than not that its pretend reason for termination is mere pretext for discrimination and retaliation.

B. COMMUNITY DANGER

Whether an employee is a corporate executive, a middle manager, or a warehouse worker, any time a company treats an employee differently because of a disabling work injury or because they reported discrimination or retaliation, that company violates the rules.

In this case, Mr. Brown suffered the indignity of Good Paper Company's supervisors harassing him for work injuries caused by Good Paper ignoring a safety issue that would have cost 60 cents in parts to fix.

Mr. Brown complained to Good Paper about the harassment, discrimination, retaliation, and intimidation.

Instead of supporting an injured employee and helping him heal, Good Paper Company allowed the harassment to escalate, ignored Mr. Brown's concerns, and fired him for a pretend reason.

This sort of corporate misconduct has no place in this community.

C. HOW DEFENDANT'S VIOLATION CAUSED HARM

Instead of complying with Mr. Brown's work restrictions and addressing his concerns about harassment, Good Paper made things worse by victim blaming, allowing the harassment to escalate, and firing Mr. Brown for a pretend reason.

If Good Paper Company had complied with Mr. Brown's work restrictions and tried to address the harassment, there is a decent chance Mr. Brown would have healed properly—physically and spiritually—and we would not be here in this proceeding today.

The second reason we are suing Good Paper and Best Paper, LLC, is that even though they admit they fired Mr. Brown for a fake reason, they have refused to meet their full accountability.

Good Paper, Best Paper, and their decision-makers are not concerned about repairing harm and restoring justice.

These corporations and their decision-makers are only concerned about denying accountability and protecting their money.

So, we're forced to bring them to trial.

IV. UNDERMINE DEFENSES

Before deciding to come to trial, we had to find some things out.

First, we had to find out whether Mr. Brown was a good worker. Because if he was a bad worker, that might explain why Good Paper fired him for a pretend reason, and not discrimination and retaliation.

So, we read his only performance review, which came out a couple of months before his work injuries, and it confirmed that Good Paper believed that he was an excellent employee who ranked 4 out of 5 in most categories.

So that's how we know Good Paper did not fire him because he was a bad worker, and it is more likely than not that discrimination and retaliation motivated the decision to fire him.

We also had to confirm that Mr. Brown was not faking his injuries and was disabled, as that term is defined under the Civil Rights Ordinance. Because if he was faking his injuries, then he has no place in this tribunal.

So, we looked at his medical records, and they confirmed that his injuries forced him to receive medical treatment numerous times for a year, including receiving two lumbar injections so he could manage his pain and get back to work.

We also looked at monthly reports from his workers' compensation QRC, who is like a workers' comp case manager. She confirmed that Mr. Brown reported that his injuries caused him intense pain, substantially affected his life, and caused him to miss work and seek medical treatment for one year.

We also talked to Mr. Brown, and he confirmed that his injuries substantially affected his ability to walk, stand, lift, do chores, and care for himself for about a year. He will testify that he has still not fully recovered from his work injuries and will probably never be the same.

That's how we know that Mr. Brown was not faking his injuries and was disabled under the Ordinance.

Next, we had to find out whether Mr. Brown was allowed to leave work without advance notice on his last day at Good Paper. Because if he was not allowed, that might explain why Good Paper now says he walked off the job.

So, we reviewed his QRC's monthly reports, and they confirmed that Mr. Brown's injuries caused him to miss around 20 days of work in 2020, but he always provided a doctor's note upon his return, and Good Paper approved all of his absences, including several multi-day absences, even though he did not always have advance permission.

That's how we know Good Paper allowed Mr. Brown to miss work without advance notice, and any contention that he walked off the job has no basis in fact.

We also had to find out whether Mr. Brown's disabling work injury and report of harassment motivated the decision to terminate. Because if either one of them did, even slightly, then Good Paper is responsible for all resulting harm under the law.

So, we reviewed Good Paper's internal documents, and they confirm that the warehouse was closed on the days it says it fired Mr. Brown for missing.

That's how we know Good Paper's reason for termination is fake, and that Good Paper's pattern of turning a blind eye to discrimination and harassment makes it more likely than not that Mr. Brown's disability and report of harassment motivated, at least in part, the decision to terminate, and that Good Paper's stated reason is mere pretext for discrimination.

Finally, we wanted to find out whether Good Paper and Best Paper, LLC, take any accountability for harming Mr. Brown and firing him for a pretend reason.

So, we listened to their decision-makers, and they told us that Good Paper and Best Paper deny any wrongdoing, that Good Paper has doubled down on how it handled things, and they sued Mr. Brown in district court in retaliation for enforcing his civil rights.

That's how we know that Good Paper and Best Paper, LLC, take no accountability and that we needed to bring them to trial to repair harm and restore justice.

V. PREPONDERANCE STANDARD

In this kind of case, you must find for Mr. Brown if the facts show he is more likely right than wrong.

Good Paper's lawyers agree that more likely right than wrong is the way you must decide. Even if you think we're just slightly more right than wrong, you'll have to find in Mr. Brown's favor.

The facts will show Mr. Brown is way more than just "more likely right."

The facts will all point to one conclusion: Good Paper let an injured worker down when it ignored his safety reports, turned a blind eye to management ignoring his work restrictions, harassed him for getting injured, and terminated him for a pretend reason that has no basis in fact.

You will hear from several witnesses and see a lot of evidence in this case. But at the end of the day, there is only one major issue you need to decide:

Is Theodore Brown a liar, a faker, and a fraud?

That is the core of the defense in this case. And if Mr. Brown is a liar, a faker, and a fraud, you should send him out of this room without a dime.

But if you decide he is telling the truth about his injuries and his harms, and Good Paper is attacking his good name to escape accountability, then your decision needs to ensure that they do not profit from this tactic.

Members of the panel, this is a straightforward case. During this trial, the facts will show we are far more likely right than wrong that Good Paper violated Mr. Brown's right to be free from discrimination and retaliation and caused him to suffer serious human injuries and spiritual harm.

We will make your decision to find in favor of Mr. Brown and against Good Paper and Best Paper, LLC, relatively easy.

VI. DAMAGES

Under the American civil justice system, the only way for Mr. Brown to enforce his civil rights was to bring a charge of discrimination. And the only way you can vindicate Mr. Brown's rights under our civil justice system is to allow him to recover money.

At the end of this trial, you must determine how much money to allow.

To figure it out, you can consider only one thing: the level of harms and losses Good Paper caused. Nothing else.

Good Paper's lawyers agree. At the end of the trial, the presiding commissioner will tell you it's the law: harms and losses only.

Everything else is out of bounds.

So, I need to talk about those harms and losses. You need to know about them as the basis for your decisions.

I'm not showing you the harms and losses to get your sympathy. Sympathy is out of bounds. You can feel sympathy, of course, but you cannot factor it into your decision.

During trial, here's what you'll hear about the harms and losses.

Mr. Brown is a decent human being. He had five children with his wife, four of whom made it to adulthood. He has several grandchildren. He has never been in trouble with the law. He was a good worker.

He is an avid sports fan and enjoyed playing them, lifting weights, and working out until he got hurt working for Good Paper Company.

Good Paper needlessly put Mr. Brown in harm's way when it ignored his request to fix the trailer truck door. It treated him like chattel after its negligence caused him to suffer serious physical injuries.

Introduction

Good Paper's management used a racial slur against Mr. Brown, forced him to perform humiliating labor outside the scope of his normal job duties that worsened his injuries, and fired him for a pretend reason just days after he reported harassment and a hostile environment.

Mr. Brown will testify that suffering the indignity of the defense's discriminatory and retaliatory treatment has had lasting effects on his dignity, self-worth, and self-esteem.

He will testify that before getting involved with Good Paper, his personality was friendly, outgoing, and fun, and that he had great relationships with his family, especially his twin daughters.

Mr. Brown will testify that Good Paper's misconduct negatively affected his personality, and that now he is standoffish and quick-tempered, and that his fiancé broke up with him and his twin girls are not currently speaking to him.

Mr. Brown's harms are ongoing, and thinking about the dehumanizing treatment the defense subjected him to, which he does all the time, triggers debilitating fear, shame, anxiety, and humiliation.

Mr. Brown will testify that having to do the type of tasks he performed for Good Paper, especially picking up boxes, triggers stress, humiliation, and anxiety, and that he did not feel this way until Good Paper violated his civil rights.

The defense's refusal to take accountability amplifies his harms.

Good Paper could have taken full accountability for how its leadership team let Mr. Brown down. Instead, Good Paper takes zero accountability, brought a retaliatory lawsuit against Mr. Brown in district court, and forced us to bring it to trial.

VII. WRAP-UP

There is no place in this community for discrimination and retaliation.

As members of this community who volunteered to enforce the Civil Rights Ordinance, it is your privilege and duty to hold a wrongdoing corporation accountable for violating another community member's rights.

The facts will show you should allow Mr. Brown to recover at least $500,000 to fairly repair harm, restore justice, and make things right.

THE PLAYERS

Darkness cannot drive out darkness.
Only light can do that. Hate cannot drive out hate.
Only love can do that.

....

MARTIN LUTHER KING, JR.

GOOD PAPER COMPANY

On the corporate side is Good Paper Company. Good Paper treated Ted Brown like a dog. They ignored him when he reported a safety issue that cost 60 cents to fix. They hurt him. They abused him. They treated him like chattel. Something less than a human.

Good Paper exposed Mr. Brown and his coworkers to serious injury. Then it harassed him, abused him, and pressured him to quit. Then it fired him for a pretend reason.

Even though Good Paper Company treated Mr. Brown like less than a human, it's not even personal. It's only about money.

TED BROWN

On the human side is Mr. Theodore Brown. Mr. Brown grew up in a college town in another state. He had a scholarship to attend the local college as a student-athlete, but he didn't go. Instead, his girlfriend got pregnant during his senior year of high school and they married. Shortly after the wedding, they moved to this state so Mr. Brown could take a factory job for a large corporation.

They divorced 20 years ago, but they still talk on occasion about family.

Mr. Brown has several grandchildren he likes to talk about, especially their college dreams. He has never been in trouble with the law. He is close to his dad, who has dementia and is in hospice care in his hometown.

Mr. Brown is 64 years old and now works low-wage temp jobs to make ends meet.

Most people like Mr. Brown don't seek to enforce civil rights. Instead, they find another job and keep living. In most cases, the civil justice system is the only way to enforce civil rights.

The civil justice system is too complicated for most humans to use. The ones who use it lose most of the time. Places like Good Paper go with corporate values and run roughshod over seldom-enforced workers' rights. Doing so increases their money profits, which is the only thing they care about.

1. The Players

Mr. Brown enforced his civil rights and brought a charge of discrimination. A charge of discrimination is a written statement signed by a human like Mr. Brown accusing an organization of discrimination and asking a government agency to do something about it. Mr. Brown said he took this action because he didn't want Good Paper to do to someone else what they did to him.

The government agencies who investigate discrimination charges dismiss over 90 percent of them.

The local civil rights department investigated Mr. Brown's charge and found in his favor.

Mr. Brown's previous lawyer represented him at a settlement conference. The case did not settle, and the lawyer withdrew from the case and sent him a $3,100 bill for services rendered. Someone encouraged the lawyer to refer Mr. Brown to me, and that's how he got my contact information.

You need a phone to schedule an appointment with me, and you also need to know how to use a calendar app. Many people who need civil rights lawyers have payment-related interruptions in their phone service or don't know how to use apps. This is how it was with Mr. Brown.

After at least two misses, we met in person at my office. Mr. Brown said he found my intake process frustrating. My process is streamlined compared to the civil justice system maze.

I believed Mr. Brown's story. I asked him to be my client, and he accepted. He said that he would go to trial to hold Good Paper accountable.

I represented Mr. Brown under a contingent fee agreement, which meant I didn't get paid unless he got paid. My fee was 40% of any money we extracted from the corporate side. I advanced case expenses, which I tried with varying success to keep under $10,000 per case in a solo practice with 20 to 30 active cases.

Mr. Brown had worked manual labor jobs for decades. The Good Paper experience left him physically and spiritually unable to do full-time manual labor.

1. The Players

At his age, he only had so many years left to work those kinds of jobs anyway.

The workers' compensation courts denied Mr. Brown's claim for permanent partial disability benefits. The courts believed Good Paper's paid expert, who called Mr. Brown a liar at his benefits hearing. If Mr. Brown retired, social security benefits would not cover his living expenses.

Mr. Brown's housing, employment, health, mobility, and domestic situations deteriorated over our 16-month engagement. He was dead broke, unhoused, and alone. He lived in survival mode.

Mr. Brown called me at least once a week for updates on his case. He desperately wanted to settle so he could breathe. Our calls always went the same way: I explained that we had to win at trial to get more than nuisance value, I told him I believed in him and his case, and he grudgingly agreed to keep going and not give up.

Mr. Brown's mounting desperation leaked out energetically and drove the corporate side to push hard for cheap justice. I felt his pain. I prayed he could hold it together through trial.

He asked me for money several times. The ethics rules prohibit client loans, but I gave him racks of cash in bunches anyway. A month before trial, I arranged a $10,000 loan from a dear high school friend that I personally guaranteed. I didn't know what Mr. Brown did with the money and didn't ask. He promised to repay after we won at trial.

The case against Good Paper was likely Mr. Brown's last chance to get enough money to retire with dignity.

THE LOCAL CIVIL RIGHTS DEPARTMENT

I liked Mr. Brown's chances. One reason was the case forum.

Local civil rights departments are underfunded and understaffed. Staff pay is low. Turnover is high. Departments do not assign investigators to most complaints. Instead, files gather dust and departments dismiss without investigation.

Mr. Brown's case was different. He filed with the EEOC, the federal agency that enforces workplace anti-discrimination laws.

The local civil rights department handled EEOC complaints within city limits. The EEOC paid the local civil rights department money for every closed case. The arrangement helped the department fund its operations and payroll. The department prioritized Mr. Brown's case.

The investigator, a former lawyer, conducted a thorough investigation. The first corporate-side defense lawyers falsely told the investigator that Good Paper fired Mr. Brown for missing shifts when it was not operating. I believe they told the investigator other untrue things, including false information about who owned the company.

1. The Players

The investigator found probable cause that Good Paper fired Mr. Brown for a false reason and discriminated against him. The rules allowed us to use the investigator's 15-page report as a trial exhibit.

Most states don't have local civil rights departments. Instead, federal laws are the only legal protections against discrimination. Federal judges dismiss between 80 and 90 percent of civil rights cases without a trial.

Mr. Brown's state has state law versions of federal anti-discrimination laws. It allows local civil rights departments to enforce these laws.

The local civil rights department held trials before a three-member Civil Rights Commission composed of three lawyers who live in the city. They volunteered to enforce civil rights and stood as judge and jury.

Civil lawsuits filed in district court take years to get to trial. The Civil Rights Commission fast-tracked Mr. Brown's case for a date-certain trial set to start about six months after the Civil Rights Department issued its probable cause finding.

The corporate side usually benefits from a thumb on the scales of justice in their favor. I believed things would be different in Mr. Brown's case.

Humans like Mr. Brown usually don't get a fair shake at civil justice. The local civil rights department leveled the playing field.

2

HARDBALL

Run through them all, from lowest to highest:
one calls for legal assistance, another comes to help;
one is on trial, another defends him, another gives
a judgment; no one makes his claim to himself, but each
is exploited for another's sake.

....
SENECA

Good Paper Company and its lawyers weren't happy about how things were going with the Civil Rights Department. So they came up with a plan to intimidate and to punish Mr. Brown for asserting his civil rights.

They filed a new lawsuit against Mr. Brown in district court, trying to make the district court take over the case and unwind the Civil Rights Department's probable cause finding of discrimination. They had no legal justification for doing this, but they did it anyway. The corporate side's illegal lawsuit against Mr. Brown included a request to make him pay them money damages, along with their costs and lawyer fees:

4.   Award ▮▮ damages, together with costs and disbursements, including costs of investigation and reasonable attorney's fees, and receive other equitable relief as determined by the court.

I filed a motion for sanctions against Good Paper on Mr. Brown's behalf.

A motion for sanctions is a request to a court (or in this case, a commission) to punish one's adversary for the way they are behaving in a legal case.

The Civil Rights Commission sanctioned Good Paper and its lawyers for suing Mr. Brown and allowed his case to proceed to trial. The Commission made the corporate lawyers pay my lawyer fees at a $400 hourly rate for my time spent on the sanctions motion.

The Commission held the corporate side accountable for breaking the rules.

This signaled that the Commission would go with human values at trial and grant Mr. Brown some real justice.

∞

External advantages such as wealth
may create more opportunities, but in themselves
they simply don't have the kind of value that
can ever define a good life.

....
DONALD ROBERTSON

INSURANCE COMPANY MOTIVES

Someone said that insurance companies drive the defense of most civil lawsuits. Even when a corporation says it's self-insured, it usually has insurance coverage.

Most insurance policies include a duty-to-cooperate provision. These provisions allow the insurance company to choose the lawyers and when to settle.

Insurance companies have little incentive to settle. They only offer to settle for way less than policy limits, regardless of the humans and harms involved.

When humans accept low settlement offers, the insurance company saves money. If humans reject low offers, the insurance company's risk stays within policy limits.

The insurance companies' goal in cases like Mr. Brown's is to delay proceedings. They understand that people like Mr. Brown are money-poor and that money-poor folk are only one calamity away from settling for cheap justice.

Insurance money decision-makers plan on humans needing to pay for calamities. For example, a human needing to pay for a health emergency needs money. Humans who need money—including their cash-strapped lawyers—feel pressure to settle for less. Accordingly, the corporate-side strategy is to starve them out. It's not personal. Actuarial tables dictate this as the most profitable thing to do, so they do it.

Delaying payment makes the insurance companies money. Instead of paying out claims, they invest the money and allow it to collect interest. The longer the delay, the greater the money profit.

∞

Never confuse movement with action.

....

ERNEST HEMINGWAY

BILLABLE HOURS

Delaying payment also makes the corporate-side defense lawyers money. Instead of settling cases, they get to continue billing by the hour.

Corporate-side defense law firms' business model depends on hourly work. Most defense law firms require lawyers to bill around 2,000 hours per year. This requires an average of about eight billable hours per workday in a fifty-workweek year.

Lawyers track billable time in six-minute increments. Six minutes equals 0.1 hours. Billable time does not include break time or any other time not spent working on client files. Most lawyers need to work at least eleven hours to bill eight hours.

The number of billable hours is the sole metric most defense firms use to evaluate lawyers for retention and promotion. Defense firms circulate a monthly spreadsheet showing each lawyer's billable hours.

Corporate defense lawyers' jobs depend on hourly work that goes away when cases settle. If several cases settle at the same time, the defense lawyers may not have any hourly work for weeks or months.

The defense firms do not adjust the billable hours quota if hourly work goes away. Instead, lawyers bill as many hours as possible when hourly work is available.

Defense lawyers feel pressure to bill hours. They contest everything to generate billable hours to keep their jobs and to earn production bonuses. They're only human.

Corporate defense lawyers need people like Mr. Brown to enforce civil rights. It allows them to bill hours, usually at $400+ per hour.

LITIGATION DELAY TACTICS

Corporate defense lawyers don't want cases to settle. The insurance companies pay them to delay proceedings. There are countless ways to delay.

They withhold documents and witnesses required by rules.

They request irrelevant documents that the rules bar them from obtaining.

They send long lists of questions called interrogatories, then they complain to the court when they don't think the human's answers are good enough. When the human sends interrogatories to the defense, the defense objects and refuses to answer.

They take day-long depositions of people who have nothing to do with the case. They get to bill thousands of dollars while forcing the human side to pay thousands of dollars for transcripts and fees. They cancel depositions at the last minute, which forces the human side to miss work for nothing, lose money, pay more fees, give up, and settle for cheap justice.

They request extensions for every hearing and deadline.

They do whatever they can to delay proceedings.

The only way to handle delay tactics is to involve the court. But even that benefits the defense lawyers, who can bill their client for time spent defending their tactics in court. The defense lawyers get to bill hundreds of hours for never-ending legal paperwork and countless court hearings.

Defense lawyers don't view their conduct as obstructionist. Instead, they believe they're only doing their jobs.

In Mr. Brown's case, the defense lawyers did all of these things, including failing to provide information about who owned the company and suing Mr. Brown in district court a month before trial.

The local civil rights department enforced rules barring obstruction. The Commission added Best Paper as a respondent in the case. It reprimanded the defense lawyers for delaying proceedings.

PAID MEDIATION AND ARBITRATION

In most cases, the defense offers to do a paid mediation in "good faith." When corporate defense lawyers say, "in good faith," what they really mean is "for cheap justice." The strategy is to get humans excited about settling. Then at the mediation, the defense only offers cheap justice. Sometimes the defense rescinds pre-mediation offers and agreed-on settlement ranges.

The humans or their lawyers must pay the mediator thousands of dollars no matter the outcome. The corporate side understands it demoralizes the human side when cases do not settle.

The corporate side seldom has to ask the human side to mediate. Instead, judges compel paid mediations with retired judges. Most mediators worked for insurance defense law firms when they were lawyers. Others are former judges who have gone on to work as highly paid lawyers for corporate law firms, capitalizing on the reputation one obtains after being on the bench. Most charge $500+ per hour to shuffle numbers back and forth over Zoom.

The mediators work with the defense lawyers to pressure the human side to settle for cheap justice. Mediations take all day and often longer. The parties sit in different physical or virtual rooms, and the mediator shuffles settlement offers and counteroffers back and forth.

Defense offers are incrementally higher than previous ones, but sometimes lower.

The longer the mediation goes on, the more hours the mediator and the defense lawyers get to bill. Meanwhile, the human misses a day of work or more, pushing him or her closer to needing to settle for cheap justice.

In Mr. Brown's case, the defense suggested a paid mediation. They would not agree to a $100,000 to $500,000 settlement range. I advised Mr. Brown that the monetary value of his harms was worth at least an amount within that range. He agreed, and we declined the offer to mediate.

The defense offered to do a private trial called arbitration. The same retired judges who do mediations do arbitrations. They sit as judge and jury and go with the defense in human rights cases around 90 percent of the time. Arbitrators charge up to $1,000 an hour and get *paid*.

We declined the offer to arbitrate.

The defense held its offer to arbitrate out to the Civil Rights Commission as a show of its good faith. It used our rejection of paid, private justice to justify suing Mr. Brown in district court. As the defense lawyer wrote in an email to the Commission:

> Good Paper has good faith defenses to this companion case that have been presented in a professional and cooperative manner. Good Paper respectfully disagreed with the probable cause finding, but attended the settlement conference with the Commission in good faith and fully intending to settle the case. Good Paper and its counsel have acted in good faith toward Mr. Brown and throughout this process. We do not believe Mr. Brown and his lawyer participated in the settlement conference in good faith. During the time allocated for claimant and respondent to

conduct private settlement discussion Mr. Brown's lawyer held up his hand and counted down from five with his fingers, counting loudly and making it clear he would not tolerate interruption. When he reached zero, he hung up on counsel, Good Paper and Rovers Insurance. Mr. Brown and his lawyer were unwilling to negotiate or even discuss this case.

Good Paper attempted to further engage Mr. Brown and his attorney in the follow-up session with you and that was similarly futile and equally offensive. Good Paper and Rovers Insurance offered significant compensation to settle, with deference to the investigator's findings, including a good faith bracket proposal that included the possibility of settlement well into the six figures. Good Paper also heard the Commission state that this process is set up for facilitating settlement and that there has not been a hearing since 2014. As a result, Good Paper offered Mr. Brown binding arbitration with an arbitrator of his choosing. Mr. Brown's response was to refuse to discuss settlement including promising you that defense counsel "believes their job is to lie and obfuscate." The entire process was unproductive, hostile, and offensive to Good Paper.

As a result, Good Paper has exercised its right to remove the case to District Court. We further believe claimant's refusal to engage in good faith negotiations and unprofessional conduct demands that a district court judge oversee this process.

∞

Energy is currency.

....

LARUSSELL

DISTORTING THE HUMAN
HELPING IMPULSE

Money and energy have become intertwined in society. I've observed that most humans treat them as one and the same.

I believe that the humans on the corporate side enjoy holding money over humans like Mr. Brown. Humans like Mr. Brown expend energy when the corporate side dangles money in front of them. The corporates take humans' energy and get off on it.

Most defense lawyers are hardworking humans. They want to validate that they are worth their $400+ hourly rates.

Nature designed humans to help others. When we help others, we can't help but help ourselves.

Corporate values distort how humans carry out the helping impulse.

Defense lawyers view themselves as zealous technicians. They believe they have a duty to use any means necessary to protect their clients' money. Going with corporate values allows them to disregard human values in discharging that duty.

They believe they are winning. They're wrong. Because another human is losing.

Humans feel a gravitational pull toward unity. Instead of promoting unity, corporatism pulls humans apart.

Like a black hole swallows the gravity of a thing, corporate values swallow the human spirit.

Corporate values lead some humans to believe that they are better and more important than others. They are wrong. We're all human. We're all made of the same stuff.

Someone said that individual humans are like limbs growing from the same tree. That each individual limb has an innate sense that what is good for the tree is also good for them.

Humans go against their nature when they elevate corporate values over human values. They cut themselves away from the tree. Too many cuts sever the connection. Trees without limbs do not grow and thrive. They wither and die.

CORPORATE JUSTICE

You have to understand, most of these people
are not ready to be unplugged. And many of them are so
inured, so hopelessly dependent on the system,
that they will fight to protect it.

....

MORPHEUS, *THE MATRIX*

While occasional exceptions exist, most judges default to corporate values and rule in favor of the corporate side on reflex. They cannot abide poor humans taking money from rich corporations. They will use the word "windfall" to describe such a situation. The implication is that a poor human does not deserve to get any more money than what is required for them to stay alive and to continue working.

Most judges would have dismissed Mr. Brown's case and denied him a trial.

Judges dismiss at least 80 percent of human rights cases before trial.

The judges in my cases dismiss even when the corporate side gets caught lying.

They dismiss when the corporate side gets caught fabricating evidence.

They dismiss because they believe written statements from corporate lawyers over live testimony from human witnesses.

They dismiss because they believe the lawyers on the corporate side over the ones on the human side.

They find that using racial slurs against subordinates does not count as illegal discrimination.

They find that leaving a hangman's noose in a Black construction worker's locker is not illegal discrimination.

They find that grabbing subordinate humans' private parts is not sex harassment.

They find that refusing to pay workers for labor isn't wage theft.

They find that kicking a 13-year-old Black human in the face who was lying prone on the ground is not excessive force. The judge compared the police officer kicking the boy, who suffered a broken orbital bone and permanent disfigurement, to children roughhousing.

They find that police entering a Black family's home on a false warrant with guns drawn is not illegal. The judge called it a mere technical violation and dismissed the case.

They find that police putting a Black woman in a headlock, cuffing her, dragging her, and detaining her is not an arrest.

They allow county jails to charge nonrefundable booking fees to innocent humans, mostly Black and brown ones. The judge said the class action lawsuit seeking refunds "completely lacked merit."

∞

The defense in cases like Mr. Brown's understand that judicial bias favors them. Their strategy is to delay proceedings and deny justice. Most judges give the defense a green light and allow it. A critical mass of judges worked at corporate law firms before they became judges. Many of them will return to corporate law firms when they have finished being judges.

Seven out of nine current Supreme Court justices lawyered at corporate law firms. Of the two who didn't, one worked for a multinational agribusiness corporation. The other one always votes in favor of corporate rights.

As a practical matter, "the law" is whatever the trial court judge says is the law. Appealing trial court judges is usually futile. Successful appeals are rare, and costly, and the process takes years. Appeals courts are affirmance machines and affirm at least 90 percent of lower courts' dismissals of human rights cases.

One district court judge reduced a jury verdict in a case where the other side's employee, a security guard, called my client the N-word and attacked him with a cane. The judge said my client should be happy to settle for less than what the jury allowed.

Another judge ordered a money-poor immigrant to accept an amount 91 percent less than the jury award for emotional damages or retry his civil rights case. The judge did not find that anyone did anything improper at trial, but he cut the "windfall" jury verdict against the corporation anyway.

Another judge threw out a verdict where a jury allowed a family to recover $10 million for a cop's wrongful killing of their son and brother. The judge, who took six months after trial to file his order, said the "patently excessive" verdict "shocked the conscience," and ruled that the maximum value of a Black human life wrongfully gunned down by a peace officer is only $2.5 million.

Several judges said in court that spiritual harms should not count as actual injuries. These judges only count economic damages as actual injuries.

Most judges compel humans to spend thousands of dollars on mandatory paid mediations with retired judge colleagues who apply pressure to settle for cheap justice.

Most judges say that the defense's request for a paid mediation is a show of good faith.

Judges know that the defense lawyers do not want to settle. They know their business model depends on hourly work that goes away if cases settle. They know that the lawyers and mediators charge $400+ per hour. They know each will bill about 12 hours for the mediation, including preparation time.

They know that if the case does not settle, the human side will still have to pay for the mediation. They know that many of the humans are money poor and living on the margins.

3. Corporate Justice

They know that the defense sets the dollar value of human injuries at zero. They know that the defense and the mediator apply pressure to settle for cheap justice.

Some judges compel humans to do up to four paid mediations before scheduling a trial.

Judges compel humans to attend routine hearings in person instead of via Zoom. Even humans who are experiencing homelessness and live thousands of miles away.

Judges deny indigent humans' requests to waive $400 filing fees in human rights cases. Even if the human is experiencing homelessness and has less than $900 to his name.

Judges order humans to give the corporate side full access to their private lives. They compel the production of things that have nothing to do with the case, such as medical and mental health records; phone, email, and social media passwords; banking and tax records, you name it.

Judges enforce subpoenas on humans' places of employment, law schools, professional schools, and trade schools. The subpoenas compel humans' employers and instructors to attend court hearings and produce full personnel files, transcripts, and other private data that has nothing to do with the case.

Judges know that the corporate side's strategy is to intimidate humans into settling for cheap justice, yet almost all of them go with corporate values and allow it.

Judges make children answer lawyers' questions about past trauma that has nothing to do with their parents' lawsuits.

These cases are real. They represent a fair sample of how judges carry out justice.

They do it like this all the time.

The district court judge assigned to Good Paper's illegal lawsuit against Mr. Brown declined to sanction the corporate side for suing Mr. Brown. He ruled that the unjustified lawsuit asking Mr. Brown to pay the corporate side damages and lawyer fees for asserting his civil rights was not frivolous.

∞

About one month after Mr. Brown's trial, a judge in a different case ordered a client experiencing homelessness to give the corporate side full access to his life. He compelled my client to produce things that had nothing to do with the discrimination case: medical and mental health records; phone, email, and social media data; call logs; text and tax records; and other private information.

The judge invited the corporate side to bring a motion for sanctions against me for declining to produce the requested information. Below is a lightly edited draft of my email to the judge.

> Good afternoon.
>
> As detailed in previous emails, corporate values—which are only about money and nothing else—have come to shape and dominate the civil justice system at the expense of human values.
>
> This case is a prime example of corporate values trumping human values, where the Court has: com-

pelled my financially destitute and homeless client, Mr. Brandon Porter, to attend a deposition in person even though he lives over 1,000 miles away, is dead broke, and everyone has done remote depositions for the past two years since the pandemic; compelled Mr. Porter to spend thousands of dollars on a paid mediation even though the process is demoralizing to people like Mr. Porter and their contingent-fee lawyers and drives them to settle for cheap justice; and granted the defense's motion to compel discovery that I believe was transparently aimed at chilling people like Mr. Porter and their contingent-fee lawyers from challenging unlawful employment practices and allowing insurance defense lawyers to hit their impossibly high yearly billable hours quota, which is routinely around 2000 hours.

This sort of thing happens all the time in my cases, and it makes me sick. So sick that I have decided to step away from the law indefinitely to heal and focus on leading with my heart after fighting for human values over corporate values for the last 15 years. Even thinking about the civil justice system makes me sick, and writing this email makes me nauseous and gives me a migraine.

In an effort to promote self-care and spiritual wellness, I am submitting this email in lieu of a more traditional response to the defense's sanctions motion, as writing more is detrimental to my health. I believe the Court has already signaled that it has made up its mind about what to do—I believe the record reflects that the Court went so far as to invite the defense to move for sanctions against me—which signals that submitting more than this is not a good use of time.

But make no mistake, I oppose the motion, as the things I wrote in previous emails show that the "objection to discovery was substantially justified [and] that other circumstances make an award of expenses unjust" under Rule 37, and refer to the emails below this one and the response my co-counsel submitted yesterday as though incorporated herein.

On a final note, I believe that this Court is biased against me and Mr. Porter because he is a Black Man experiencing homelessness and because the insurance defense lawyer is a white woman who represents the corporation. I will clarify that I have no reason to believe the Court's bias is malicious. Instead, I believe the Court has been conditioned to elevate corporate values over human values.

We all have.

Two weeks later, the judge sanctioned me for $11,000.

In most cases, there is neither malice nor mean spirit behind how judges do their jobs. Instead, corporatism conditioned them to elevate corporate values over human values.

From corporate bias flows outcomes that benefit the corporate side to the detriment of the human side.

3. Corporate Justice

Corporate justice.

Corporate justice explains why judges dismiss at least 80 percent of human rights cases.

Most judges want to get it right. Most judges believe corporate justice is getting it right.

Most judges are so inured to corporate justice, they are incapable of rational thought about it. They perceive straightforward descriptions of corporate justice as derogatory, personal attacks.

Yet most judges feel on a limbic level that corporate justice is out of balance with human nature.

They treat humans like files instead of like humans as a way of getting out of feeling guilty.

Most judges find it jarring and unnatural to call corporate justice what it is.

Corporate justice impedes judges' ability to see the corporate side for what it is and to treat it as it deserves.

Some say that courts are de facto corporations.

Justice delivered with care grounds society during hard times like an oak holds its ground in a storm.

Corporate justice uproots.

How things are in society shows how good the humans in charge of justice are at their jobs.

Corporations' influence on society exceeds that of any government or nation.

Corporate justice grows their influence.

TORT REFORM

Information is the currency of democracy.

....

THOMAS JEFFERSON

The corporate community started the tort reform movement in the 1970s. Its goal is to program jurors to view monetary compensation for human injuries as offensive.

By using the word "reform," with its implication of moral improvement, the corporate community tries to prevent humans from thinking critically. They get humans to falsely believe that corporate values should trump human values.

Tort reformers falsely portray the human side as survival threats to jurors in these kinds of ways:

1.   Lawsuits undermine the quality and availability of health care for your family.

2.   Lawsuits ruin the local economy. They threaten jobs and thus endanger your ability to feed and house yourself and your family.

3. Lawsuits make everything more expensive. They take money you need to care for your family.
4. Lawsuits suppress the development of new products that keep you and your family safer.
5. Lawsuits endanger religion. Plaintiff's lawyers donate money to liberal politicians, who appoint liberal judges. Liberal judges hate God, force teaching evolution, and permit abortions and gay marriage.

Tort reformers also falsely portray the humans bringing lawsuits and the lawyers who represent them as greedy liars looking for a windfall.

Most jury pools are tort reformed.

Courts in Mr. Brown's state assemble jury pools of about 20 to 30 people for civil trials. Six sit on the jury and one or two alternates attend trial but do not deliberate on verdicts. The judge dismisses some prospective jurors for reasons like health, childcare, or clear bias.

Court rules disallow lawyers from telling juries about how the corporate side operates. Insurance coverage, claims adjusters, reserves, lowball settlement offers, and billable hours quotas are all off limits.

Instead, lawyers can identify tort-reformed jurors by asking questions during jury selection.

Jury selection happens before opening statements. Each side gets to strike two jurors from the pool for any reason except a discriminatory one. In trials where the plaintiff is non-white, the corporate side usually strikes non-white jurors. Most judges allow it.

The text below are lightly edited notes from a seminar I presented about working with juries in human rights cases. The bullet points are jury selection questions from real trials.

Emotional harm in general - No advocacy at this point. You have no credibility with a tort-reformed jury, and it is way too early to advocate or even attempt to "educate" the jury.

- Does anyone think it's possible for someone to suffer genuine emotional harm even if the harm does not cause them to seek treatment from a mental health professional or miss work?
- Have any of you been retaliated against because you opposed discrimination? Tell me about that.
- What kind of conduct do you think should count as retaliation?
- Do any of you have a family member who was retaliated against because they opposed discrimination? Tell me about that.

Bad Facts - If there's a fact a jury might find bad for your case, you might want to bring it up during jury selection to inoculate the jury against the other side beating its chest about it.

- This is a disability discrimination case. Some folks, like my gramma, think that as long as you have

two arms and two legs and can talk, you're not disabled. One of my good friends has a kid who has
two arms and two legs and can talk, but he's got
a learning disability and gets special accommoda-
tions at school because he's considered disabled
under the law. How many of you are more like my
gramma as far as what should count as a disability? Tell me more about that.

- What kinds of impairments do you think should
  count as a disability?
- Do any of you have disabilities or have had a temporary disability before? Tell me about that.
- Do any of you have a family member who has a disability or has had a temporary disability before?
  Tell me about that.

**Tort Reform – You want to address this stuff head-
on. Not just to make challenges for cause and peremp-
tory challenges, but to get the jury talking and potentially persuade each other.**

- Some people say the law requiring a jury to allow
  damages should have a maximum amount, no
  matter what the facts of the case show. Others feel
  there should be no maximum and the jury should
  allow the full amount of the harms and losses.
  How many of you are closer to feeling there should
  be limits on the amount the jury allows? Tell me
  your thoughts about that.

4. Tort Reform

- How many of you feel jury verdicts against a private business can hurt the economy in this community? Tell me your thoughts about that.

- Some people think that juries should not be permitted to allow damages for emotional harm. Some people are okay with it. Which side are you closer to? Tell me your thoughts about that.

- How many of you feel jury verdicts against a private business can make things more expensive for everyone in the community? Tell me your thoughts about that.

- Do you think less of the plaintiff because he has filed a lawsuit?

- How many of you here would never sue another person? Tell me your thoughts about that.

- Some people believe there are too many lawsuits. How many of you believe that's true? Tell me your thoughts about that.

- Some people believe that lawsuits are costing us too much money. How many of you believe that's true? Tell me your thoughts about that.

- Some people believe that jury awards are often too high. How many of you believe that's true? Tell me your thoughts about that.

- Do you believe it is the justice system's responsibility to protect people from harm? Tell me about that.

∞

Some courts draw juries from rural counties where most residents voted for Donald Trump whenever they could. Tort reform has taken hold within this group.

Mr. Brown's trial didn't have a traditional jury. Instead, a panel of city-dwelling lawyers who volunteered to enforce civil rights stood as judge and jury.

Even though the humans who sat on the panel in Mr. Brown's trial were all white, I believed those city-dwelling volunteers would reject tort reform and allow someone who looked like Mr. Brown to recover a full vindication for his spiritual harms. I thought they would go with human values over corporate values.

5

JUSTICE DELAYED

It is a small part of life we really live.
Indeed, all the rest is not life but merely time.

....

SENECA

GOOD FAITH

Good Paper had a $500,000 liability insurance policy that covered Mr. Brown's case. The policy had a $100,000 deductible that required Good Paper to pay expenses and lawyer fees up to $100,000.

The policy allowed the insurance company to choose the lawyers and when to settle. Insurance companies have a legal duty to give equal consideration to the insured's interests.

The corporate side only offers to settle for cheap justice in cases like Mr. Brown's. The goal is to keep the amount of lawyer fees plus the settlement payment below the deductible. Doing it this way makes the insured pay the entire cost of defense and the insurance company pays nothing.

Insurance companies rarely offer more than $10,000 in cases like Mr. Brown's. Forcing people like Mr. Brown to choose between cheap justice and going to court chills other people from enforcing their rights and protects the insurance company's money. Sometimes they allow the lawyers to bill up to 80 percent of the deductible before offering to settle.

CHEAP JUSTICE

Good Paper harmed Mr. Brown, denied accountability, and took him to trial.

The defense's trial strategy in cases like Mr. Brown's is always the same. I knew they would bad-mouth him, victim-blame him, put shame on his name, and call him a liar.

Good Paper's conduct had lasting effects on Mr. Brown's self-esteem, self-worth, and dignity. Some call these soft or emotional distress damages. Others call them human injuries.

In some states, including Mr. Brown's, human injuries are compensable with no caps. Refusing to take accountability counts as ongoing compensable harm.

Most juries that allow compensation for human injuries tie the amount to economic damages. For example, if a jury allows $20,000 for economic damages, it will only allow $20,000 for human injuries.

In Mr. Brown's case, we would not request money for economic damages. Instead, we would only request the jury to allow money for Mr. Brown's human injuries.

The corporate side valued Mr. Brown's human injuries as zero.

We needed to win at trial and get a judgment on the verdict to elicit more than a cost-of-defense settlement offer.

OPPORTUNITY

Winning at trial is only part of the process of getting justice. Collecting judgments on verdicts can be the hardest part of the case. Getting the corporate side to pay a judgment is a process that starts before trial.

The first step is sending what defense lawyers call a demand letter. Others call them settlement opportunity letters.

A trial lawyer I admire explained how it works in a treatise he authored about settling cases.

Every case has a reserve set by the insurance company claims adjuster. This is the amount the insurance company sets aside to pay a potential judgment. The insurance company does not want to set high reserves. The law requires them to hold reserves in a cash account that doesn't earn interest.

Setting reserves low allows the insurance company to put more money into interest-earning accounts to maximize money profits.

Insurance companies take in trillions of dollars in monthly premiums from their customers and then deny coverage whenever they can get away with it. This allows them to invest or earn interest on this extra money. Insurance companies make billions of dollars in profits.

Insurance companies are also masters at paying less than what they set aside and earning interest on the difference.

Insurance companies hate paying more money than they planned to. They will not pay more for a case than the amount in reserves. Instead, they invest the money and allow it to collect interest. They use defense lawyers to delay payment, often for years.

Delaying payment makes the insurance companies money profits. The longer the delay, the greater the money profit. Delay makes the insurance defense lawyers more money. They get to continue billing by the hour.

Remember how judges will often refer to a large award of money to a poor human as a "windfall?" Judges would never use the word "windfall" to describe the huge amounts of money that insurance companies or insurance defense lawyers get from delaying payment.

People like Mr. Brown often give up, and the insurance company pays no one except lawyers.

Courts often reverse plaintiffs' verdicts and the insurance company pays no one except lawyers.

5. Justice Delayed

Even if people like Mr. Brown win at trial and get a judgment, the corporate side won't pay. They only pay if enough reserves were set aside to cover the judgment. Instead of paying, they continue to delay.

Settlement isn't the main objective of the settlement opportunity letter. Instead, the aim is to maximize pressure on the corporate side. Doing so is the only way to get them to set the reserves high enough to cover a judgment.

Ethics rules prohibit direct communications with represented parties, so I had to go through the lawyers to talk to the insureds and claims adjusters.

My first goal of a settlement opportunity letter is to pressure the corporate defense lawyers.

The defense lawyers don't want cases to settle. Many won't share settlement offers with the claims adjusters or the insured, even though the lawyer ethics rules require lawyers to share settlement communications with their clients.

Of the ones who do, most only share the dollar amount of the offer with the claims adjuster and nothing else. Pressure is the only way to get the lawyers to loop in the claims adjuster and the insured.

The second goal of the settlement opportunity letter is to get the insurance company to set reserves high. Claims adjusters set reserves. They get a bonus if the reserves are low and the payout is less. The less the payout, the higher the bonus. The goal is to pay nothing.

If the payout is large the claims adjusters get no bonus, but they get to keep their job so long as the payout is less than the amount in reserves. Payouts way higher than the reserve amount put their jobs in jeopardy.

Insurance companies have a legal duty to set reserves, usually in the first 90 days of getting a claim. In cases like Mr. Brown's, most claims adjusters set reserves based on a report from the defense lawyer.

The defense lawyer has billable hours requirements, so he or she has an incentive to recommend a low reserve. This makes a settlement less likely and guarantees future billable hours.

Once reserves are set, most insurance companies will not reevaluate for at least one year, if ever.

Even when the human side wins at trial, the corporate side refuses to pay judgments on jury verdicts all the time. The corporate side will continue trying to persuade the human side to settle for cheap justice, threatening endless appeals and delays, or using corporate shell games to claim that there is no money to pay the judgment.

This post-trial email from the defense in a different case where a jury allowed my client to recover money from her former employer for wrongfully terminating her shows how it goes when reserves are too low:

> Hi Human,
> This confirms that in response to your January 18, 2023 offer of $250,555.88 (the judgment amount), I made a counteroffer of $180,000 earlier today, on

5. Justice Delayed

January 20, 2023. You responded by increasing your offer to $260,000.

So, I want to summarize our telephone conversation from a few moments ago. I called you so you could explain to me the basis for the increase in your settlement demand if ACME, INC. did not pay before the deadlines you set out in your January 18 offer (you did something similar on November 30, 2022, when you made a settlement offer of $240,000, with a deadline to accept of 4:00 p.m. on December 7, 2022. You also indicated that if that offer was not accepted before the deadline, the offer would increase to $250,000 and then increase an additional $10,000 on the first of every month thereafter until the matter resolved or the outcome of any appeal).

Today, you began by telling me that "Yesterday's price is not today's price." When I asked you to further explain the basis for increasing your settlement from the judgment amount, you told me there is a consequence to not paying the offered amount.

You also indicated that even if ACME, INC. paid the judgment amount today, your client would not accept less than $260,000. When I asked why, you said that if ACME, Inc. paid less than $260,000, your client would not agree to confidentiality, non-disparagement, or a release, as well as indicating that you would not recommend that your client sign a satisfaction of judgment. You also repeated your earlier statement that "yesterday's price is not today's price."

I suggested to you that the court would likely not enforce your offer/demand. You then acknowledged that "theoretically" we could bring a motion and have the court force your client to sign a satisfaction of judgment. You also told me that if I made another counteroffer, your client's offer would increase to $270,000.

You further told me that for $260,000, I could "get my client out of this," with confidentiality, non-disparagement, and a release. I responded by telling you I could get my client out of this by paying the $250,555.88 judgment, and that your $260,000 offer was "made up." At that point, you said this conversation "had reached a point of diminishing returns" and you did not want to talk anymore. You then hung up.

The corporate defense lawyer likely billed at least $200 to write that email. The claims adjuster in that case likely set reserves at zero or close to it.

Reserves would always be too low to cover judgments if left to the lawyers and the claims adjusters.

Indeed, when I signed up Mr. Brown, I was fighting to collect multiple unsatisfied judgments on my clients' jury verdicts and hadn't gotten paid in a year.

Under bad faith laws, insurance companies who reject offers below policy limits risk paying the entire judgment. Including amounts greater than policy limits.

Some judges apply corporate justice to bad-faith laws. They only require the insurance company to pay judgments that exceed policy limits up to the amount of the last offer rejected.

In all my cases, I wrote settlement opportunity letters lacking in Chesterfieldian politeness. I called the insurance adjusters and defense lawyers out for what they are. I exposed the frivolous defenses. I pointed out conflicts of interest. I drove wedges between the insurance adjusters, the lawyers, and the insureds. I flipped the script.

I bullied the bullies.

The letters changed the game. I sent them via email. Some of the letters made it past the defense lawyers and on to the claims adjusters and the insureds. The corporate side paid judgments on old cases and settled early in new ones.

In Mr. Brown's case, the corporate side did not offer to settle for more than the cost of defense.

Here are the lightly edited settlement opportunity letters from Mr. Brown's case:

SETTLEMENT OPPORTUNITY LETTER #1

APRIL 1, 2022

Good morning, defense.

SETTLEMENT OPPORTUNITY

Please consider this an offer for the $500,000 insurance policy limits as full resolution of this matter. Please immediately forward this by email to Good Paper Company and Its Successors in Interest, GPC Operations LLC, All Insurance Companies that Have or May Have an Interest in this Case, All Insurance Companies that May Provide Coverage to Satisfy All or Part, of any Judgment in This Case, All Real Parties in Interest, and All Money Decision-Makers.

LIABILITY

Mr. Theodore Brown recently retained me. My understanding is that before I got involved in this case the defense belittled his harms and walked out of a mediation with the Local Civil Rights Department, even though the Department had already conducted a thorough investigation of his Charge of Discrimination and issued a detailed, 15-page report finding probable cause that the defense subjected him to illegal discrimination and retaliation.

Perhaps the defense was posturing. If not, its conduct signals that whoever is driving the defense's litigation strategy has not thought through how badly things will go for it if this case proceeds to a trial before a panel composed of Civil Rights Commissioners.

In case you have not already read the LCRD's probable cause memorandum, please do so. Here is a link to it on Dropbox: https://www.dropbox.com/s//xxxxx

The memorandum is a scathing indictment against the defense and will come in at trial. *See Smith v. City of Springfield*, XXX F.3d XXX, XX (8th Cir. 2000) (confirming that a probable cause finding was admissible under the rules of evidence and immunized discrimination claims from summary judgment).

5. Justice Delayed

The probable cause finding will be more than enough to prove that the defense is liable for discriminating against Mr. Brown for getting injured at work and firing him in retaliation for complaining about the hostile work environment, including a GM calling him the N-word and a shift supervisor punishing him in retaliation for getting injured by making him lift 120 boxes that weighed close to his exact weight lifting restriction in quick succession.

Has the defense thought about how it will discredit the Civil Rights Department's probable cause finding to a panel of City residents who volunteered to be on the Civil Rights Commission formed to protect civil rights?

What will the defense arguments look like?

Will the defense suggest that the Department is biased? That the Department got it wrong and that the defense is more credible? The defense will have little to no credibility with the panel given that its stated reason for termination is a sham, specifically, that it fired Mr. Brown for missing work on days when its facility was not even open, as detailed in the probable cause memorandum.

Will the defense argue that the 15-page probable cause memorandum is not sufficiently thorough? These defenses are weak and the panel will reject them.

Will the defense instead admit that it discriminated and retaliated against Mr. Brown? Doing so may keep the probable cause memorandum out at trial but it will enrage

...u give my side the green light to ask for record damages.

Will the shift supervisor who punished Mr. Brown for getting injured by making him lift 120 heavy boxes in a row offer trial testimony helpful to the defense? That is not going to happen.

Will the HR Manager who fired Mr. Brown for missing work on days when the facility was not even open offer credible testimony that the termination was all a big misunderstanding and not discriminatory and retaliatory? That is not happening, either. There is nothing anyone can say at trial to improve the defense's chances.

After the panel hears the defense deny wrongdoing in a case with clear liability and listens to the defense try to walk back the sham reason for termination, it will allow Mr. Brown to recover an amount in damages that represents full justice. If the defense's trial strategy is to badmouth Mr. Brown and try to put shame on his good name, the strategy will backfire and the panel will likely allow him to recover a record amount in damages for this kind of case.

I have seen it happen over and over again in my cases where the defense badmouths my client, lies, obfuscates, and does everything it can to escape accountability, and at trial the jury sees through the mendacity and punishes the defense with verdicts in my clients' favor.

DAMAGES

Mr. Brown is a decent human being. He has four grown children and several grandchildren who are a part of his life. He has never been in trouble with the law. He enjoys sports and enjoyed playing them, lifting weights, and working out until Good Paper Company's negligence caused him to suffer serious physical injuries. He was a good worker, as detailed in the probable cause memorandum the panel has likely already studied.

Good Paper Company needlessly put Mr. Brown in harm's way when it ignored his request to fix the trailer truck doors at its facility that kept falling open on their own, and treated him like chattel after one of the doors he complained about fell open and hit him, seriously injuring his neck, back, and head.

The defense used racial epithets against Mr. Brown, forced him to perform humiliating labor outside the scope of his normal job duties as physical punishment for getting injured that exacerbated the work injuries caused by the defense's negligence, and fired him for a pretend reason several days after he complained about a hostile work environment.

Mr. Brown will testify that the defense's discriminatory and retaliatory treatment has had lasting effects on his dignity, self-worth, and self-esteem.

Under the law the defense must pay Mr. Brown money damages for all harms caused by its civil rights violations, including future emotional harms.

Mr. Brown's harms are ongoing, and even thinking about the dehumanizing treatment the defense subjected him to, which he does all the time, triggers debilitating fear, shame, anxiety, and humiliation. The fact that the defense refuses to take accountability amplifies his harms. *See W.J.R. v. Peter*, No. A18-0613, 2019 WL 12345678, at *5 (XX. Ct. App. Apr. 20, 2019) (recognizing that a defendant's denials of misconduct and wrongdoing may be ongoing sources of compensable emotional harm).

Mr. Brown will credibly testify that having to do the type of tasks he performed for the defense, especially picking up boxes, triggers stress, humiliation, and anxiety, and that he did not feel this way until the defense violated his civil rights.

Spiritual energy and wellness are priceless. But since the civil justice system requires us to put a dollar value on Justice, Justice must never come cheaply.

If I have to try this case I will suggest to the panel that Mr. Brown's compensatory damages are equal to at least $1,000 for each of the 120 boxes the defense made him lift in a row as punishment for getting injured at work and $200 for every box he lifts going forward that triggers the human injuries the defense caused him to suffer as an insult to the serious physical injuries caused by its negligence.

5. Justice Delayed

Will the defense argue to a jury that these are unreasonable amounts for compensating the needless loss of Mr. Brown's spiritual energy and wellness, which is priceless? Take a walk outside and reflect on it. Are these amounts unreasonable? Or are they reasonable given that money is the only form of Justice available to Mr. Brown.

Mr. Brown waives his right to recover economic damages. Even if a jury only allows him to recover cheap justice, the defense will still have to pay up to $300,000 for his attorney fees. *See, e.g., Jerkins v. Univ. of XX*, No. CV 13-1827, 2017 WL1234567, at *1 (allowing around $300,000 in attorneys' fees and $20,000, in costs in a fee-shifting case where the jury allowed $1.00 in damages); *XXXXX v. XXXXX,* 14-CV-1234, 2016 WL 1234567 (finding that plaintiff's counsel Human Lawyer's reasonable hourly rate is equal to $335); *XXXXX v. XXXXX*, 555 N.W.2d 555, 555 (2019) (on remand, the jury allowed Human Lawyer's client to recover an amount well into six figures for "garden-variety" emotional harm damages); *XXXX v. XXXXX.*, 555 (2021) (the jury allowed Human Lawyer's client to recover around $500,000 in "garden-variety" emotional harm damages and found that Human's reasonable hourly rate is equal to $400).

EXPIRATION

This settlement opportunity expires on December 1 at 5 PM and must be accepted in writing. The offer will automatically increase by $20,000 on the first of every month until this matter resolves. Any request for an extension of this offer will constitute a rejection.

The defense and its money decision-makers should consider the wisdom and risk of continuing to throw money at defending this case, as litigation costs are likely already at or near $30,000 and will likely cost the defense at least another $150,000 to litigate to trial, and another $100,000 to $200,000 to appeal a verdict with no guarantee of a win. These amounts do not include Mr. Brown's fees and costs, which the defense will have to pay under the Civil Rights Ordinance if the defense loses at trial.

I have won my last five civil jury trials, including two employment trials and three total in the last year, and my juries allowed my clients to recover millions of dollars. The last two times my adversaries dug in their heels and forced me to take cases to State Supreme Court, I won there too.

The last time the defense belittled a client's harms and walked out of a mediation in one of my civil rights cases, it signaled that this sort of vibe would leak out at trial and that things would go poorly for the defense. Things ended up going very poorly for the defense, and the jury allowed my client to recover around $400,000 in non-economic damages for his human injuries.

As a courtesy here are links to the verdict form and order for judgment from that case:

https://www.dropbox.com/s//xxxxx
https://www.dropbox.com/s//xxxxx

5. Justice Delayed

Please add that case and the other recent cases I have taken to trial and won (available online via this link: XXX) to the past precedent database the defense uses to evaluate its risk.

The defense has a fiduciary duty to inform Good Paper Company, the insurance carriers, and the money decision-makers of the risks involved in refusing to settle for a reasonable amount, and that includes telling them whom you are dealing with. I suggest that you ask Retired Judge XXX from XXXX County District Court or Retired State Supreme Court Justice XXX about the work I have done and the results I get.

I say these things not to brag but to put the defense and its money decision-makers in a position to properly evaluate its exposure. When the jury allows Mr. Brown to recover a verdict for an amount that represents full justice, I will file this settlement offer in support of a fee petition for $400 an hour, the hourly rate the court allowed me to recover in my last case where the defense disagreed with me about the money value of my client's human injuries and risked going to trial.

The panel in this case will grant the fee request in full when it sees that the defense had an opportunity to settle for partial justice but instead risked exposing itself to a six-figure verdict with pre- and post-judgment interest accruing at 10 percent per annum, and six figures in plaintiff's attorney fees available under the Civil Rights Ordinance. $300,000 is a reasonable floor for the defense's exposure, not including defense attorneys' fees which will be deep into six figures.

If this demand is not paid, please make sure that at least $3 million in reserves are set aside to cover a judgment, which is a reasonable estimate of the defense's exposure if this case proceeds to trial given the availability of noneconomic damages (potentially seven figures), statutory attorney fees (well into six figures) and pre- and post-judgment interest (into six figures).

I have a track record of going the distance for my clients—and winning. This is the defense's best opportunity to resolve this matter before damages and attorney fees significantly increase and the final outcome is left to the hearts and minds of a panel composed of City residents who volunteered for and were selected to be on a Commission dedicated to advancing civil rights.

In case you have not already looked up the Commissioners who will sit on the public hearing panel please do so:

Presiding Commissioner XXXX: https://www.dropbox.com/s//xxxxx

Commissioner XXXX: https://www.dropbox.com/s//xxxxx

Commissioner XXXX: https://www.dropbox.com/s//xxxxx

A trial will be a disaster for the defense. This is not a case where the defense wants to dig in its heels and litigate. Refusing to save money by settling for partial justice now will look like an even worse decision in hindsight to the panel and the defense's final money decision-makers when they read this email predicting how things would go and see that the defense took a needless gamble and went to trial.

Please feel free to call me on my personal cell phone to discuss this settlement opportunity if you find it unclear in any way 555.555.5555.

In compliance with the Presiding Commissioner's Order, I confirm that I am currently available on the following days for a prehearing conference: April 5, 6, 8, 9, 12, 13, 15, 22, 23, 30.

—*Human Lawyer*

SETTLEMENT OPPORTUNITY LETTER #2

MAY 10, 2022

Good afternoon, defense.

Please immediately forward this settlement communication to Good Paper Company and Its Successors in Interest, Good Paper Co-owners XXXX and XXXX, GPC Operations LLC, Rovers Insurance Company, Rovers Insurance

Company Claims Adjuster XXXX, All Insurance Companies that Have or May Have an Interest in this Case, All Insurance Companies that May Provide Coverage to Satisfy All or Part, of Any Judgment in This Case, All Real Parties in Interest, and All Money Decision-Makers.

Today's Zoom prehearing conference was a disaster for the defense. The Presiding Commissioner rejected all of the defense's requests regarding the scope of discovery, confirmed that the Commission will require the defense to respond to Mr. Brown's discovery requests (including providing the name of the entity that will have to satisfy a judgment), admonished defense counsel for his misconduct, and confirmed that defense counsel's contention that when the defense loses the trial in this case it will get to appeal the Commission's decision to the district court with de novo review is wrong.

If the defense had done its research, it would have known that the State Administrative Procedures Act governs judicial review of panel decisions and provides for review to the Court of Appeals, not the district court. The Court of Appeals confirmed that the defense's notion about how appeals work is dead wrong when it affirmed a panel decision of the Civil Rights Commission in *Fire Department v. Colfax*, XXX N.W.2d XXX, XXX (Ct.App. 2010):

"An agency decision is presumed correct and is not reversed unless one of several statutory bases is met. In relevant part, we only reverse agency action when the

finding, inferences, conclusion, or decisions are … un-supported by substantial evidence in view of the entire record as submitted; or … arbitrary or capricious…We defer to agency credibility determinations, lest[we] substitute [our] judgment for that of the agency." (citations and quotations omitted).

Today's hearing confirmed that the defense and its legal team have little credibility with the Commission, and that a trial will be a disaster for the defense. This email confirms that Mr. Brown has increased his settlement offer to $520,000, and it will automatically increase by $25,000 on the first of every month until this matter resolves.

The defense's main argument when it was trying to persuade Mr. Brown to settle his claims for cheap justice when the Presiding Commissioner was off camera was that the panel was the equivalent of a junior varsity tribunal and that it would get to bring an appeal in front of the district court with de novo review.

Now that the defense knows it is dead wrong on the law and that an appeal will go to the Court of Appeals who will "**defer to agency credibility determinations, lest [we] substitute [our] judgment for that of the agency**", it should recalibrate its litigation strategy and get its insured, Good Paper Company and its successors, out of this case as soon as possible instead of risking the very serious consequences of a money judgment accruing at 10 percent per annum, and before it bleeds more of Rover's money on what is shaping up to be a very bad loss for the defense.

If the defense refuses to settle, the $500,000 insurance policy, which it needs to disclose to me next month per the Commission's instructions, will likely not be enough to cover a judgment in this case, especially given the availability of statutory attorney fees. Please make sure that at least $3.5 million in reserves are set aside to cover a judgment, which is a reasonable estimate of the defense's exposure if this case proceeds to trial given the availability of noneconomic damages, statutory attorney fees, pre- and post-judgment interest, and the defense's lack of credibility with the Commission.

Also, please make sure that the insured, Good Paper Company, and its successor in interest (whom I will know the identity of once the defense provides discovery responses), has its own separate counsel — *a verdict against Good Paper will make it and potentially its principals responsible for satisfying a judgment.*

Independent, personal counsel will be able to advise Good Paper whether the insurance company and its appointed lawyer are fulfilling their fiduciary duties to act in the best interests of the insured by advising it to reject a reasonable offer within policy limits and exposing them to the risk of a substantial judgment, and whether that advice is negligence.

If the defense continues to play hardball and does not settle, then I believe Good Paper may have a bad faith claim against Rovers Insurance for failing to accept Mr. Brown's previous reasonable settlement offer within policy limits, and I can recommend XXXX as potential bad faith counsel: https://www.dropbox.com/s//xxxxx

At bottom, if Good Paper has not retained a separate, independent lawyer to evaluate this settlement opportunity, I suggest it finds one immediately, as the one the insurance company appointed made no friends with the Commission today, and does not even know something as basic as how appeals work in this sort of a case.

Things went very badly for the defense today and they are only going to get worse. Refusing this settlement opportunity now will look like a worse decision in hindsight when the panel allows record damages for this kind of case.

Please feel free to call me on my personal cell phone to discuss this settlement opportunity if you find it unclear in any way: XXX.XXX.XXXX"

—Human Lawyer

SETTLEMENT OPPORTUNITY LETTER #3
MAY 17, 2022

Good afternoon, defense.

Please immediately forward this settlement communication to Good Paper Company and Its Successors in Interest, Good Paper Co-owners XXXX and XXXX, GPC Operations LLC, Rovers Insurance Company, Rovers Insurance Company Claims Adjuster XXXX, All Insurance Companies that Have or May Have an Interest in this Case, All Insurance Companies that May Provide Coverage to Satisfy All or Part, of Any Judgment in This Case, All Real Parties in Interest, and All Money Decision-Makers.

Please consider this a settlement offer for $600,000 as full resolution of this matter.

Whoever is driving the defense's litigation strategy does not know what they are doing. First, the defense confirmed that it does not understand how appeals work under the Civil Rights Ordinance, as detailed in previous emails, and now it brought an impermissible lawsuit against Mr. Brown in district court asking the Court to find probable cause as a matter of law that the Department lacked probable cause to find probable cause.

In other words, it sued Mr. Brown to collaterally attack the Department's findings, and indeed the authority of the Civil Rights Commission itself.

Not only is the lawsuit impermissible and frivolous, which exposes the insured, Good Paper Company, and its successors and possibly its principals and its lawyers to Rule 11 sanctions, it needlessly exposed them to a counterclaim under the Civil Rights Ordinance, which bars any person from "engaging in any retaliation, economic or otherwise, because another person opposed a discriminatory act forbidden under this title, has filed a charge, testified, assisted or participated in any manner in an investigation, proceeding or hearing under this title."

Under the Ordinance, "person" includes "one or more individuals, labor organizations, partnerships, associations, corporations, legal representatives, mutual companies, joint stock companies, trusts, unincorporated organizations, trustees, trustees in bankruptcy, receivers, public bodies or public corporations, any other legal or commercial entity, and any agent or employee of all the foregoing."

Under the Ordinance, "retaliation includes, but is not limited to, any form of intimidation, retaliation, or harassment."

The insured, Good Paper Company, and its successors and possibly its principals and its lawyers, sued Mr. Brown in district court for opposing a discriminatory act forbidden under the ordinance, filing a charge, and participating in a contested case proceeding. Good Paper Company and its successors and possibly its principals and its lawyers are therefore liable to Mr. Brown for retaliating against him by suing him.

The defense's liability under the Ordinance for retaliation by the frivolous lawsuit is significant given the availability of non-economic damages and attorney fees.

This case will go in front of the Commission for a trial on the underlying probable cause finding. The defense's litigation stunts will go over poorly with the Commission. Has the defense thought of how upset the Commission will be with the defense for forcing it to do extra paperwork that it does not get to bill $400 an hour for? The volunteer commission dedicated to advancing civil rights will not take kindly to that at all.

The defense made no friends with the Commission during the December 30 hearing and this frivolous lawsuit will further undermine its credibility. Did the defense hear the tone in the Presiding Commissioner's voice when she admonished defense counsel for his repeated interruptions? It was brutal. Did the defense see the look on the Presiding Commissioner's face when the Rovers Insurance Claims Adjuster referred to her by her first name? Ice cold.

The trial will be a disaster for the defense. The defense keeps making unforced errors and driving up its exposure. $600,000 is a reasonable floor for its exposure.

At this point, it is imperative that the insured, Good Paper Company, and its successor in interest and principals have their own separate, independent counsel—*a decision against Good Paper will make it and potentially its principals responsible for satisfying a judgment.*

If the defense does not settle, then I believe Good Paper and its successor in interest, and principals may have a bad faith claim against Rovers Insurance for failing to accept this settlement offer and for bringing this frivolous lawsuit.

Please call me on my personal cell phone if the defense finds this settlement opportunity unclear: 555.555.5555

—*Human Lawyer*

SETTLEMENT OPPORTUNITY LETTER #4
JUNE 17, 2022

Good morning, defense.

Please immediately forward this settlement communication to Good Paper Company and Its Successors in Interest, Good Paper Co-owners XXXX and XXXX, GPC Operations LLC, Best Paper LLC, Rovers Insurance Company, Rovers Insurance Company Claims Adjuster XXXX, All Insurance Companies that Have or May Have an Interest in this Case, All Insurance Companies that May Provide Coverage to Satisfy All or Part, of Any Judgment in This Case, All Real Parties in Interest, and All Money Decision-Makers.

Please consider this a Rule 68 total-obligation offer and demand for $650,000 as a full and complete resolution of this matter.

Last week Rovers Insurance Claims Adjuster XXXX sent me an email regurgitating a cliff's notes version of the defense's untimely position statement drafted by the previous insurance carrier-appointed lawyer from the insurance carrier's previous law firm.

He also recapped the defense's version of settlement discussions, and laid out the defense's vision of "good faith" settlement negotiations (i.e., ones that give it the best chance of settling for cheap justice). Yet Rovers' Insurance Claims Adjuster XXXX asked me to respond to his pointless email to defense counsel. Everything about Mr. XXXX's email was off-brand.

My co-counsel, Mr. Sidney Aurelius Slaughter, suggested that the aim of the email was to bait me into responding to a represented party so the defense could bring sanctions motions against me and an ethical complaint, too.

I told him I did not think the defense was that low or that desperate, as Mr. Brown's legal claims are so rock-solid and the defense has behaved so poorly that this case is a layup that could probably try itself in front of the Commission.

Perhaps the defense hoped to settle for an amount less than the insured's deductible and that Rovers would have to pay little money, if any, to resolve this case.

Perhaps Rovers Insurance hoped that the amount of defense fees billed by its appointed lawyers, Defense Counsel Ms. XXXX, Defense Counsel Mr. XXXX, and Defense Counsel Mr. Sidney Aurelius XXXX, would be an amount less than the insured's deductible and that Rovers would have to pay little money, if any, for defense attorney fees to resolve this case.

Perhaps Rovers Insurance, Rovers Claim Adjuster XXXX, his appointed lawyer XXXX and the defense's legal team hoped to settle this case for cheap justice and leave the insured party, Good Paper Company, and potentially its principals and successors in interest, XXXX, XXXXX, and XXXXX, on the hook for everything.

5. Justice Delayed

The defense's litigation blunders, as detailed in previous offers, have exposed the insured party, Good Paper Company, and potentially its principals and successor in interest, Best Paper, LLC, to a judgment far exceeding policy limits and put them on the hook for hundreds of thousands of dollars.

Complainant/Defendant Brown served the defense with sanctions motions in district court and with the Commission for bringing an illegal lawsuit against Mr. Brown for enforcing his civil rights with the EEOC and the Civil Rights Department.

The Court and the Commission will grant those motions and allow Mr. Brown to recover his attorney fees and severely sanction the defense, its lawyers and potentially its money decision-makers and potentially its principals and successor in interest, Mr. XXXXX, Mr. XXXXX, and Best Paper Co., for suing someone for getting a probable cause civil rights determination in his favor.

Defendant Brown has a motion to dismiss in district court teed up and ready to file. The Court will grant it, along with the sanction motions, and forever extinguish the wild notion that the defense was allowed to unilaterally remove this case to district court and divest an authorized Civil Rights Department's jurisdiction.

The Commission may allow the case to proceed on damages only as sanctions for the defense's refusal to comply with the Presiding Commissioner's Order to show up for depositions and otherwise participate in proceedings. The Presiding Commissioner and the other Commissioners, all City residents who volunteered to be on a board dedicated to advancing civil rights, will allow Mr. Brown to recover record damages for this kind of case, way more than the policy limits. As detailed in the probable cause finding, Good Paper Company's General Manager called Mr. Brown the N-word, treated him like chattel, and fired him for missing work on a day when its plant was not even open because of a Covid closure.

The defense's illegal, retaliatory lawsuit against Mr. Brown violated his rights protected under the Civil Rights Ordinance. The defense's Rambo lawsuit against Mr. Brown gave rise to another retaliation case against the defense, its lawyers, and potentially its money decision-makers and potentially its principals and successors in interest. That new case is coming down the pike.

The defense's exposure is way more than policy limits. The defense has exposed its insured, Good Paper Company, and potentially its principals and successors in interest to a judgment greater than the policy limits collecting interest at 10 percent per annum that they will be on the hook for and have to pay.

The defense has resorted to having the claims adjuster send meaningless emails that may be aimed at trying to lure me into ethics violations as a Hail Mary attempt to save its case.

If the defense is really that desperate and if this is the sort of amateur-hour strategy we can look forward to at trial, please confirm so and I will advise Mr. Brown to authorize me to increase his settlement offer to $1 million.

The defense should accept the offer, put this case to rest, and avoid needlessly risking its insured, Good Paper Company, Best Paper, LLC, and potentially their money decision-makers and potentially their principals and successor in interest to record judgments in two cases.

Please feel free to call me on my personal cell phone if this offer is unclear in any way: 555.555.5555.

—*Human Lawyer*

SETTLEMENT OPPORTUNITY LETTER #5
JUNE 23, 2022

Good afternoon, defense.

Please immediately forward this settlement communication to Good Paper Company and Its Successors in Interest, Good Paper Co-owners XXXX and XXXX, GPC Operations LLC, Best Paper LLC, Rovers Insurance Company, Rovers Insurance Company Claims Adjuster XXXX, All Insurance Companies that Have or May Have an Interest in this Case, All Insurance Companies that May Provide Coverage to Satisfy All or Part, of Any Judgment in This Case, All Real Parties in Interest, and All Money Decision-Makers.

Please consider this an offer for $700,000 as full and complete resolution of this matter.

Last week the Commission issued an order severely sanctioning the defense and its lawyers for bringing an illegal lawsuit against Mr. Brown.

As the Commission put it:

The Commission concludes that Respondent's assertion before the Commission that proceedings before the Commission are subject to an automatic stay pursuant to Section XXXX is sanctionable under Rule 11. The facts before the Commission strongly suggest that Respondent is using this novel maneuver in an effort to delay the proceedings before the Commission and to intimidate or harass the Complainant.

The Order is a disaster for the defense. Here is a link to it: https://www.dropbox.com/s//xxxxx

The Commission made the defense lawyers pay Mr. Brown's lawyer fees incurred opposing Respondent's illegal attempt to divest the Commission of jurisdiction. As it appears that Mr. XXX, Mr. XXXX and the money humans behind the insured corporations have been paying all the defense lawyer fees up to this point and getting nothing but problems to show for it, I believe that they should consider requesting the Commission to make the Fisch & Benson law firm and Rovers Insurance claims counsel Mr. XXXX reimburse them for their fees incurred as a result of Respondent's illegal Rambo lawsuit against Mr. Brown and assertions of removal and automatic stay before the Commission.

5. Justice Delayed

The Commission also granted Mr. Brown's request to amend his charge to add a retaliation claim under the Civil Rights Ordinance against the defense for bringing the illegal lawsuit against him.

Yesterday Mr. Brown formally amended his charge to include an additional count of retaliation under the Ordinance against Respondent Good Paper Company; its lawyers, Fisch & Benson, Mr. XXXX, Ms. XXXX and Sidney Aurelius XXX; and Respondent's decision-makers, as identified in Respondent's discovery responses, dated June 13, 2022: Mr. XXX, Co-Founder, XXXX, Inc.; Mr. XXXXX, Co-Founder, XXX, Inc.; Mr. XXXX, Claim Counsel, Rovers Insurance.

Mr. Brown will testify that when he found out that the defense lawyers, Fisch & Benson, Mr. XXXX, Ms. XXXX, Mr. Sidney Aurelius XXX, and, apparently, the insurance claims counsel, Mr. XXX, sued him in retaliation for enforcing his civil rights, he was on a Greyhound bus headed out of state to visit his dying father in hospice. The defense's conduct caused him to suffer humiliation, anxiety, and stress, and amplified the existing humiliation, anxiety, and stress he was already dealing with from the underlying litigation.

The defense and its lawyers have zero credibility with the Commission. The Commission will allow Mr. Brown to recover hundreds of thousands of dollars for his spiritual injuries in connection with his new retaliation claim, along with the hundreds of thousands of dollars it was already going to allow him for his underlying claims.

This case is turning into one disaster after another for the defense.

Apparently, defense lawyer Mr. XXXX and Rovers Insurance Claim Counsel Mr. XXX are the ones at fault.

This email confirms that if defense lawyer Mr. XXXX confirms in writing to the Commission, the Department, and the Complainant's lawyer via email by noon on June 30, 2022, that he and Rovers Claim Counsel Mr. XXX were the ones who decided to sue Mr. Brown and assert removal and automatic stay before the Commission, then Complainant Brown is agreeable to pursuing his additional retaliation claim against the lawyers and the insurance company only.

At this point, I believe it is imperative that the insureds have their own separate, independent counsel— *a decision against Good Paper will make it and potentially its principals responsible for satisfying a judgment.*

I believe that the conflicts on the defense's side are numerous, and I believe that not advising the insureds to obtain their own separate, independent counsel may constitute bad faith.

Independent, personal counsel will be able to advise Good Paper and its principals whether Rovers Insurance, Rovers Insurance Claims Counsel Mr. XXX, and Mr. XXX's appointed lawyers are fulfilling their fiduciary duties to act in the best interests of the insureds by advising them to reject reasonable offers within policy limits and exposing them to the risk of a judgment, potentially advising them to reject Complainant's offer to allow the additional retaliation claim to proceed against the lawyers and the insurance company, and whether that advice is negligence.

Please call me on my personal cell phone if the defense finds this settlement opportunity unclear: 555.555.5555.

If Good Paper Company and the humans behind it and its successors in interest obtain personal, independent counsel, I encourage independent counsel to call me on my personal cell phone to discuss potentially getting their clients out of this case.

—*Human Lawyer*

The corporate defense lawyers in Mr. Brown's case complained that my settlement opportunity letters were unprofessional. Lawyers in other cases also complained about them.

A lawyer from another case filed a formal ethics complaint against me over a settlement opportunity letter similar to the ones from Mr. Brown's case. The ethics board ruled that my letter counted as professional misconduct and admonished me. I appealed.

The board held the appeal hearing several days after Mr. Brown's trial at the state Supreme Court building in my state's capital city.

The ethics lawyer I hired told me to show up for the hearing dressed like a lawyer. I wore a black muumuu.

I testified in my defense at the hearing. One of the three panelists asked me if the allegedly unethical settlement opportunity letter was a one-off. I told him that I sent loads of them because they usually helped my clients.

I testified that the corporate side in the underlying case had delayed paying my client for months and finally paid shortly after I got involved and sent a settlement opportunity letter.

I testified that my client was a money-poor, 67-year-old black grandmother who was her grandchildren's primary caregiver. The corporate side in that case, a property management company, subjected her to illegal housing discrimination that caused her to experience homelessness and her teenage grandson to miss the first week of school. I testified that she wanted to settle her case so she could give her grandkids a special Christmas.

The panel deliberated for about 15 minutes and affirmed the admonition against me. This was not the first permanent blemish on my law license.

As of this writing, the ethics board hearing where I lost my appeal was my last court appearance as a lawyer. Perhaps my *last* last.

6

ROOTS

The evils of capitalism are
as real as the evils of militarism and racism.
The problems of racial injustice and
economic injustice cannot be solved without
a radical redistribution of political
and economic power.

. . . .

MARTIN LUTHER KING, JR.

Corporations, money and nations
exist only in our imagination. We invented them
to serve us; why do we find ourselves sacrificing
our lives in their services?

. . . .

YUVAL NOAH HARARI

Corporatism played out to its logical extreme in Mr. Brown's case. I believe corporatism is a virus that causes humans to malfunction. I believe that America, the birthplace of modern race-based slavery, is ground zero.

Early 1600s: Corporations settle America
to make money profits.

King James of England chartered the Virginia Company in 1606 to colonize America. Virginia, named after Queen Elizabeth, stretched from present-day Maine to the Carolinas.

The Virginia Company was one of the first corporations. Corporations protected investors with limited personal liability in case of money losses. In other words, money profits for investors were theoretically unlimited, while money losses were limited to the amount of the investment.

The goal of the Virginia Company was to make money profits by growing cash crops like sugar and tobacco.

The Virginia Company established the General Assembly, the first colonial government in America. It was the driving force behind race-based slavery for money profits.

Europeans had African slaves before colonizing the Americas. They enslaved non-Christians for centuries but did not target Africans. Slave status was not for life or based on skin color. Instead, a slave of any skin color could become free by converting to Christianity.

The first colonists did not think of themselves as "white" or use that word to describe themselves. They saw themselves as Christians or Englishmen, or by their social class. They were nobility, gentry, artisans, or servants.

For much of the 1600s, the American colonies operated as agricultural economies. Indentured servants did the work. Most workers were poor, unemployed laborers from the English working class. Like others, they traveled to North America for a better life.

Africans and poor whites stood on the same ground. Black and white women worked side-by-side in the fields. Black and white men who broke their servant contract received equal punishment. Europeans and Africans worked together, intermarried, had children together, and ran away together.

There were all kinds of mixed-race families and children in early colonial times.

They shared resentment toward the well-to-do Virginia corporates who ran the government. They all had servitude contracts for a certain length of time, often seven years.

They received food and shelter, a basic education, and sometimes a trade in exchange for labor. After their servitude, they earned "freedom dues." These usually included a piece of land, supplies, and a gun. Black-skinned or white-skinned, they became free.

Former indentured servants began to pose a threat to the property-owning corporates.

The Virginia General Assembly placed restrictions on available lands. This amplified unrest among former indentured servants. Workers of all skin types participated in a series of violent uprisings. The unrest culminated in an open rebellion in 1676 when they burned down Jamestown, the colonial capital.

Late 1600s to 1700s: The corporates who run the American colonial government start race-based slavery to maximize money profits.

*White Americans must recognize that justice
for black people cannot be achieved without radical
changes in the structure of our society.*

....
MARTIN LUTHER KING, JR.

Armed former indentureds of all skin types far outnumbered the Virginia elites. The Virginia corporates saw the indentured system unraveling. They looked to divide the labor force to control it. Stressing cultural and ethnic divisions was a way to do that.

Racial slavery was a better way for the Virginia leaders to maximize money profits. It was easier to keep track of slaves, especially ones you could identify by skin color. Slaves identified by skin color couldn't move on and become free competitors.

The Virginia leaders made the brown ones slaves.

The Virginia General Assembly wrote the shift to race-based slavery into law.

They changed the definition of who could be a slave from non-Christian to non-European.

They changed the law from saying that Black humans *could* be slaves to saying that they *should* be slaves. One

Christian pastor observed that the words "Negro" and "slave" had become interchangeable.

They changed the law to say that Black humans would be slaves forever.

The Virginia slave owners gave poor whites new privileges and status over black slaves. They made them plantation overseers and slave catchers. They drove the two groups apart by skin color and made it less likely that they would unite again in rebellion.

No matter how wide the gap between rich and poor, whites eased class tensions among themselves by emphasizing skin color. They told themselves that whites were a "superior race." Some told themselves they were doing God's work taking care of what they believed was an inferior people.

Controlling the slave population concerned all European-descended whites, regardless of slave ownership status.

Slavers created patrols to squash slave rebellions and catch runaway slaves. They used excessive force and terror to control slaves. Slave patrols were a model for police forces, who still use slave patrol tactics.

Vigilante militias patrolled roads and enforced slave curfews with violence and murder. The South resembled a police state.

Until America, modern humans only based slavery on religion, status, capture during a war, or debt.

For the first time in modern human history, a society branded humans as chattel for life based only on skin color.

Corporatism led humans to race-based slavery to maximize money profits.

By the Revolutionary War, the transformation to a race-based slavery society was complete. Virginia, rooted in corporatism, led the way.

Race-based slavery was an injustice that went against nature.

Early to Mid-1800s: Race-based slavery for money profits makes slave owners the richest humans in America.

Tobacco was the colonies' main cash crop until the Revolutionary War. Britain bought less American tobacco after the war and growing it was not profitable. Slave owners started growing more of another cash crop, cotton.

Picking and cleaning cotton took a long time and was not profitable until the invention of the cotton gin in 1794. By 1850 cotton made up half of all U.S. exports. Slavers bought and sold millions of African slaves and expanded west. European slave traders made massive amounts of money on African slaves.

Black human slaves picked cotton in sweltering heat from sunup to sundown six days a week. Overseers used whips and violence on slaves to coerce faster picking.

6. Roots

Black slaves ate food that slavers found unfit for animals. They lived in small shacks with dirt floors and little or no furniture. Slave owners sold slaves' children and spouses to faraway plantations for breeding and cotton picking. Rape and torture were common. Millions of Black slaves lived in survival mode.

Race-based slavery was the backbone of the American South's economy. Slaves became a legal form of property. Slaves were a major source of tax revenue for state and local governments, which also taxed slave sales. Slaves were the slavers' most significant money investment and the bulk of their wealth.

There was no paper currency in circulation during slave times. Banks invented papers that allowed Southern slavers to use slaves to pay off debt and to pay for things.

Black humans were money.

By the start of the Civil War in 1861, the South was producing 75 percent of the world's cotton. The Mississippi River valley had the most millionaires per capita in the nation. If the South had been a separate country, it would have ranked as the fourth richest in the world at the start of the War.

Southern money wealth was all tied up in slavery. Support for it in the South was rock solid.

1861 – 1865: Civil War for money profits makes the North a world economic power.

Many Americans, especially in the North, and especially women, opposed slavery and sought to end it. Slavers dug in their heels in support of slavery. They argued that it was necessary for American economic survival and for slaves' own good. They said that Blacks were not mentally suited to take care of themselves and needed masters to do so.

Abraham Lincoln was not on the ballot in 10 southern states and won the 1860 presidential election anyway. This signaled to Southerners that their way of life did not have a future in America.

The South seceded in early 1861 and created the Confederate States of America. The Confederacy went to war against the Union right away.

Some say that the American Civil War was less about ending slavery to advance moral authority and more about maximizing money profits.

The South was almost all rural and agricultural. The slavers who ran the South had no incentive to change the system. The money and culture were all tied up in Black human slaves.

In the North, the colder climate disfavored growing cash crops on massive plantations. Instead, northern corporates brought machines and raw materials together. They built factories and mills with assembly lines. Low-wage workers produced clothes, shoes, furniture, guns, ammo, you name it.

6. Roots

The northern corporates did not use unpaid slaves for labor. Instead, they used low-wage labor from a massive, steady stream of European immigrants.

Some have said that poor factory workers could sometimes be treated worse than slaves. A slaver does not want his slave to die, because to replace the dead slave costs him money. To replace a dead factory worker costs no money at all. Corporate values.

With the South out of the picture, Congress passed laws that Southerners had blocked for years.

New laws allowed the United States government to colonize the West. Other ones allowed it to issue paper money not backed by gold or anything else. The government spent free money on industry, infrastructure, and war.

During the second year of the war, Congress passed the Homesteading Act. The Act granted land about equal to the size of California and Texas combined to settlers for free. Millions settled on land where millions of humans already lived. The settlers helped the government develop agriculture, exploit resources, and fight the locals.

Before the war, only private banks issued paper money. Instead of paper money, the United States used gold and silver coins as official currency. Congress made laws allowing the United States to issue paper money and making it illegal to refuse the paper money as legal tender.

Instead of using Black human slaves as money, the union issued millions of green paper notes that fit in a pocket.

President Lincoln said Congress should not add "In God We Trust" to the fiat currency. Instead, he joked, "If you are going to put a legend on the greenbacks, I would suggest that of Peter and Paul, 'Silver and gold I have none, but such as I have I give to thee.'"

President Lincoln's observation shows that money is an abstraction and only exists in humans' imaginations. "Real" money has the same intrinsic worth as pretend Monopoly money: none.

The North's massive wartime spending grew its economy. Northern and British banks made big money off loans to northern corporations. Way more than they ever did off of loans to southern slave owners to buy land and slaves.

Late 1800s: "Black Code" laws push former slaves into "slavery by another name."

There was scarcely a white man in the South
who did not honestly regard Emancipation as a crime,
and its practical nullification as a duty.

....

W.E.B. DUBOIS

6. Roots

The South's economy was all tied up in slaves and collapsed when it lost the war. New laws ended slavery, made former slaves citizens, and gave Black men voting rights.

Some northerners wanted to enforce the new civil rights laws. They believed former slaves should have equal opportunities.

But the North didn't enforce the new civil rights laws. It failed to provide freed slaves with political or economic support.

As a result, 90 percent of former slaves stayed in the South working on plantations as sharecroppers. Within less than a generation, former slave-owning families recovered most of their wealth.

Southern laws called "Black Codes" made it illegal for former slaves to own land and work most jobs. Freed former slaves had no food, housing, or money. There was nowhere for freed slaves to go or work. For most, there was only one option: sharecropping, which many call "slavery by another name."

Former slaves who lacked schooling entered into sharecropping contracts with their former owners. They worked and lived as tenants on the same plantations they had worked as slaves. Men worked in the fields, while some women worked in houses as maids and cooks. Sharecroppers' children were part of the contract and worked by their parents' side.

Instead of housing and food, sharecroppers received a share of the crops. The arrangement tied them to land, which they worked on leased equipment. They bought seeds, fertilizer, food, clothing, supplies, and anything else the land didn't provide on credit at high-interest rates.

They lived, ate, and dressed the way they had as slaves.

Black Codes made it illegal for sharecroppers to sell crops. They prevented sharecroppers from moving if indebted to their landlords. When harvests failed, sharecroppers went into debt. The debt carried over until the next year. And the next.

White supremacist groups and law enforcement were often one and the same. They used violence, apprehension, detention, and murder to enforce the Black Codes. They pushed sharecroppers into a system called convict leasing.

Bounty hunters, often former slave catchers, used force to arrest indebted sharecroppers. They arrested other Black people for petty crimes like vagrancy and stealing food.

Companies and individuals paid fees to state and local governments for convict labor. Black prisoners convicted under Black Codes worked plantations, mines, lumber yards, brick yards, factories, railroads, and road construction. Some picked cotton in the same fields they worked as slaves and sharecroppers. None received payment for their labor. Convict leasing made money for Southern governments and former slavers. It drove the rebuilding and modernization of the South.

Many Black people moved away from the Black Codes to cities in the North and Midwest in search of a better life. Many Black migrants experienced violence and racism just as bad as in the South.

Institutionalized segregation and discrimination trapped former Black slaves and their descendants in a cycle of debt and poverty lasting for generations.

The slave went free; stood a brief moment in the sun; then moved back again toward slavery.

....

W.E.B. DUBOIS

Late 1800s to 1920s: Corporatism and foreign wars make members of the American corporate community among the richest humans in the world.
Northern leaders did not focus on the legacy of slavery. Instead, they focused on expanding west. They built railroads and slaughtered the humans whose ancestors had lived near the tracks for generations to the edge of extinction.

The U.S. economy continued to grow after the Civil War. Corporations, fueled by limited liability and limited government regulation, led the way.

The Supreme Court ruled in 1886 that private corporations are natural persons. Corporations gained the rights and benefits of persons without the responsibilities of personhood.

The corporate community made massive profits off exploiting anything in nature. Mountains, plains, trees, plants, animals, minerals, gasses, oils, water, lakes, rivers, humans, children, diseases, you name it.

Judge-made corporation law requires corporations to prioritize money profits for shareholders over everything else. A famous court case, *Dodge v. Ford Motor*, shows how it works.

In *Dodge*, Henry Ford wanted to use corporate profits to add jobs and increase workers' wages. Investors in Ford Motor Company called shareholders sued him for not using profits to pay them a dividend.

The Court held that Ford had a duty to prioritize money profits to shareholders over everything. It made him pay shareholders a massive amount of dividend money instead of increasing jobs and wages.

The Dodge brothers who sued Ford used their dividend payout to build up their competing car manufacturing business.

Going forward, shareholders used courts and the threat of lawsuits against corporations to ensure that corporations prioritized shareholder profits over everything.

Money went from being *a* thing to being *the* thing.

Corporate factories made weapons for U.S. soldiers fighting wars against brown-skinned locals in the West and around the world.

Everywhere the military went, it protected and enforced corporations' money investments and profits. The

U.S. war machine stretched the country's borders from coast to coast. It extended them to tropical islands in faraway longitudes and latitudes.

United States Marine Corps Officer Major General Smedley Darlington Butler fought in most of the wars from this era.

He started his 34-year career in 1898 when he lied about his age to join the military. He fought in the Philippine–American War, the Boxer Rebellion, the Mexican Revolution, World War I, and several other wars, incursions, and conflicts.

At the time of his death, Butler was the most decorated Marine in U.S. history. By the end of his career, he had received sixteen medals, including five for heroism. He is the only Marine to receive the Brevet Medal and two Medals of Honor, all for separate actions.

After Butler retired from the military, he became an activist. He spoke out and wrote against war profiteering, including this:

> I spent 33 years and four months in active military service and during that period I spent most of my time as a high-class muscle man for Big Business, for Wall Street and the bankers. In short, I was a racketeer; a gangster for capitalism. I helped make Mexico and especially Tampico safe for American oil interests in 1914. I helped make Haiti and Cuba a decent place for the National City Bank boys to collect revenues in.

I helped in the raping of half a dozen Central American republics for the benefit of Wall Street. I helped purify Nicaragua for the International Banking House of Brown Brothers in 1902–1912. I brought light to the Dominican Republic for the American sugar interests in 1916. I helped make Honduras right for the American fruit companies in 1903. In China in 1927 I helped see to it that Standard Oil went on its way unmolested. Looking back on it, I might have given Al Capone a few hints. The best he could do was to operate his racket in three districts. I operated on three continents.

Early 1930s: U.S. corporate leaders plan a coup to overthrow the president with a fascist dictator.

The U.S. economy plunged in 1929 when the stock market crashed and lost about 90 percent of its value. The crash led to massive money losses on Wall Street. Drought and soil mismanagement led to crop failure and massive money losses on Main Street. The Great Depression set in.

Massive amounts of workers in every part of the country lost jobs and homes. By 1932, about a quarter of all Americans and half of Black ones were out of work.

Franklin Roosevelt, a Democrat, won the presidency in 1932. He blamed the Depression on unchecked corporate corruption, speculation, and greed. The day after taking office, he shut down the Wall Street banks for a week. He made corporate leaders sit for public congressional hearings and testify about their business practices.

He pushed through what he called New Deal laws. The New Deal took power from corporations and gave it to government agencies. It passed with votes from white southerners, who voted in a solid Democratic bloc since the Civil War.

Many Black humans expected the New Deal to have Jim Crow parts to it given that white Southern Democrats made and enforced racist Jim Crow laws.

While racial discrimination was a problem with parts of the New Deal, some programs benefited Blacks. As the New Deal progressed, more Black folk found their political voice. They pushed for racial justice and equal opportunities. They joined unions and interracial leftist coalitions. Most switched from voting for Republicans to Democrats.

If most Blacks voted for Democrats, it would ensure Roosevelt's reelection.

Many in the corporate community believed Roosevelt shamed them for doing their jobs. They believed he shamed them for following the law: prioritizing money profits.

They believed the country was on a dangerous path toward communism. They thought the communists would take their money.

To protect their money, they plotted to overthrow Roosevelt with a fascist dictatorship.

The corporate leaders involved in the plan ran corporations that were household names. Government leaders and military generals were also involved.

Fascism is a kind of society where an authoritarian government ruled by a dictator controls the lives of the people. Fascist governments use violence to suppress people who disagree with them. Italian Benito Mussolini came to power in 1922 and was the first European fascist leader. Adolph Hitler became the second when the Nazis took control of the German government.

White supremacy was a defining part of European fascism. Hitler said that pale skin, blond hair, and blue eyes marked a master race. He said that Jews, Gypsies, and Blacks were inferior and a threat to Germany.

Fascism appealed to many corporate leaders. It was about prioritizing corporate profits over human values. It was about wiping out equal opportunities, unions, and interracial leftist coalitions.

The corporate community got behind European fascism early. At least one big American corporation gave a massive loan to the Italian fascists in the 1920s.

Plenty of big American corporations funded the Nazis in the 1930s. Famous corporate leaders openly supported Nazi dictator Adolf Hitler.

In 1933 a group of corporate leaders recruited General Smedley Butler to be a fascist dictator. They asked General Butler, a famous war hero, to help them overthrow the government.

6. Roots

They chose the wrong guy. While General Butler spoke out against war profiteering and mistreatment of war veterans, he believed in democracy. He went along with the plan to figure out who was behind it and expose them.

A year later, a congressional committee investigated rumors of the plot. Most believed the plot was a hoax, but General Butler came forward to testify about it. General Butler, whose life and career support his credibility, laid out the plan.

The corporates modeled the plot on how Mussolini came to power in Italy.

Corporate leaders would select a popular war hero to be the face of a fascist movement. The face would first rally veterans and then the masses behind it.

General Butler was a charismatic public speaker. He was popular with veterans as a decorated soldier and champion of veterans' rights.

Corporates targeted veterans as a group dedicated to patriotism and trained for violence.

They wanted General Butler to lead a massive group of veterans in a March on Washington. They believed such a show of force would pressure Roosevelt to step down like the King of Italy had.

The corporates wanted General Butler to be their white knight and take orders from them. They offered him money and power. General Butler went with human values and exposed the plot.

A classified, internal committee report confirmed that General Butler told the truth. As the committee co-chair put it, "Powerful wealth is concentrating for its own preservation."

President Roosevelt acknowledged the plot when he said in a speech, "It was natural and perhaps human that the privileged princes of these new economic dynasties, thirsting for power, reached out for control over government itself...In their blindness they forget what the flag and the Constitution stand for."

Several years after General Butler's testimony, the Nazis started World War II. This put to rest the corporate community's plans for a fascist coup.

1940s to Present: Corporatism becomes the dominant influence on humans and the environment.

The problem of the twentieth century
is the problem of the color-line.

....

W.E.B. DUBOIS

The U.S. government spent massive amounts of money on World War II. Corporations made massive money profits from factories, especially ones that made military equipment.

6. Roots

Wartime planning and spending lifted the United States out of the Great Depression and grew the economy to new heights. While New Deal programs had targeted human beneficiaries, wartime spending went in the first instance to corporate interests.

World War II-era corporations did not rely on slave or low-wage immigrant labor. Instead, they benefited from a massive, steady stream of unemployed Black migrants from the South.

A New Deal program paid southern farmers subsidies *not* to plant crops. The plan was to help the farmers by driving up crop prices. An unintended consequence was eliminating the farming jobs Black Southerners relied on.

Millions of Blacks lacking education and skills migrated north for jobs in the 1940s.

Employers didn't consider them equal to whites. New Black migrants competed with earlier Black migrants for jobs and wages.

White employers only hired new migrants to the lowest-paying jobs. This set up competition between Black workers and kept wages down.

Higher unemployment and low wages deprived the descendants of Black slaves of equal opportunities. Lack of opportunities kept them in a cycle of debt and poverty.

As one U.S. Senator summarized: "Entire legal structures were created to prevent African Americans from building economic security through home ownership.

Legally enforced segregation. Restrictive deeds. Redlining. Land contracts. Coming out of the Great Depression, America built a middle class, but systematic discrimination kept most African-American families from being part of it."

Whites left cities for the suburbs. For every Black entering a northern city, almost three whites left. Whites left because they didn't want Black neighbors and thought that more Blacks would lead to them paying higher property taxes.

Thus began a generation of prosperity and economic growth for whites as the United States dominated the world economy.

The price that America must pay for the continued oppression of the Negro and other minority groups is the price of its own destruction.

....

MARTIN LUTHER KING, JR.

In 1960 more than half of U.S. Black men worked manual labor jobs. Only two percent of women and Black men had professional jobs. Ninety-four percent of doctors in the U.S. were white men.

That disparity protected rich white men. Discrimination and corporate justice devalued everyone else as humans and workers.

Congress passed laws in the 1960s aimed at eliminating poverty and racial injustice. Many corporate community members believed the country was on a path toward socialism. They thought that a socialist government would take their money.

The corporates made long-term plans to elect officials and judges who embraced their values. They secured financing from wealthy donors. They established networks of academics, capitalists, economists, journalists, and politicians worldwide.

The corporate community had its candidates and judges in place by the 1980s. They transformed almost every aspect of life into an unregulated free market. Everything was for sale to the highest bidder without consideration of human values.

They used drug laws with increasingly harsh sentences to warehouse millions of young Black men in prison. Those men would come out of prison with felony records, preventing them from securing jobs or decent housing.

They busted trade unions and eliminated safety regulations. They lowered taxes for the wealthy. They shamed and vilified poor Blacks, inventing racist caricatures like the "Welfare Queen." They used this as justification for terminating social welfare programs. They transferred money to the super-rich and eliminated trade regulations.

Corporatism requires limitless economic growth through the consumption of products. The corporate community used the media, especially television commercials, to create consumers.

They converted America from a needs culture to a desires culture. They groomed people to desire new things before they consumed old things. They programmed people to care more about their desires than needs. As an early corporate marketer put it:

> [T]he conscious and intelligent manipulation of the organized habits and opinions of the masses is an important element in a democratic society. Those who manipulate this unseen mechanism of society constitute an invisible government that is the true ruling power of this country. We are governed, our minds molded, our tastes formed, our ideas suggested, largely by men we have never heard of... In almost every act of our daily lives... we are dominated by the relatively small number of persons ... who pull the wires which control the public mind.

The corporate community pushed the message that humans are individualistic and only care about money. They took it for granted that corporatism is the best way to organize humans. As a British Prime Minister put it: "There's no such thing as society. There are individual men and women and there are families."

The corporate community tightened its control of government, finance, business, and the media. They spread corporatism around the world.

Corporatism's dominance widened inequality gaps and further concentrated money wealth. For example, the world's 25 or so richest people own as much wealth as half the entire world's population.

A global network helped corporations gain more power than any government or nation. They became the dominant force in shaping human activity on the planet.

Judges applied corporate justice and removed legal limits on corporations' growth and business practices.

Big corporations get bigger through mergers and acquisitions. Massive multinational corporations stamp out competitors and set their own terms. About 70 percent of the hundred largest economies in the world are corporations.

Cities and countries compete against each other to attract corporate investment. They waive taxes, zoning and environmental codes, and worker protection laws for corporations. The corporations then swoop in to extract the benefits of the legal system, schools, and other infrastructure in those places.

Multinational corporations control most of the world's finance, manufacturing, agriculture, and trade. Countries invite them to take part in international treaty negotiations to protect corporate interests. In most countries, corporations and governments are one and the same.

Corporations around the world have one goal: maximizing profits. Most humans in the twenty-first century live in societies organized around money.

Corporations are veterans of over a century of shareholder lawsuits. They are experts at prioritizing money profits over everything. Each year corporations make massive money profits by monetizing human activity and nature with no regard for human values.

∞

Corporations would be psychopaths if they were real, natural persons.

Psychopaths lack care or empathy for the harm caused by their actions.

I believe psychopathy is symptomatic of corporatism. Corporatism has infected most humans.

I believe it made the humans on the corporate side in Mr. Brown's case treat him how they did at his job and in the courtroom. They are devoid of care or empathy for the harm they cause in pursuit of money profits.

┌─────┐
│ 7 │
└─────┘

TRIAL

Injustice anywhere is a threat to justice everywhere.

....

MARTIN LUTHER KING, JR.

Mr. Brown's trial was a spirit-injurious farce. The corporate side treated him so badly during trial that I decided before it was over that I was done trying cases. I refused to put another human through the kind of abuse that the corporate side piled on my friend Mr. Brown.

Below in bold, italicized text are lightly edited notes of my closing argument from Mr. Brown's trial.

Good afternoon. We brought hardball litigation to the Commission on Civil Rights.

The two-day trial was the first trial the Commission held in 12 years.

Thank you, Commissioners. Why are we even here? What just went on here?

This case is about corporate values v. human values.

It's not personal. It's not even about Mr. Brown or anyone else in the room. It's not personal. It's just about money. You all saw the defense finally start to squirm at the end of this trial when the money papers came out.

The money papers were the last exhibits from the trial. These official corporate filings came in as impeachment evidence against Good Paper's corporate representative.

He testified that Good Paper sold the company to an out-of-state corporation, Best Paper, and was out of business. He described the transaction as an "asset purchase" whereby Best Paper allegedly purchased the assets of Good Paper but assumed no liabilities.

Money judgments against empty vessels like Good Paper are worthless.

The money papers showed that Good Paper and Best Paper are intertwined companies. They also showed that the Good Paper corporate representative is Best Paper's CEO.

Corporation law allows parent companies to play what some call a "shell game" or "three-card monte." They create separate entities for different parts of the company and strip mine it when it may be liable for some harm it may have caused.

Spinoff corporations declare bankruptcy to avoid judgments. The parent corporation keeps doing business as usual and pays nothing. The corporate owners pay nothing.

7. Trial

A legal doctrine called veil-piercing prohibits using shell corporations to avoid judgments. Judges seldom apply it.

The corporate side objected to the money papers coming in. The Commission denied the objection and admitted the papers as evidence.

The corporates demanded a recess. They turned red, sweated, loosened their ties, and hurried out of the courtroom. They huddled in corners to make phone calls and type text messages.

Under bad faith laws, the insurance company would have to pay a judgment against Best Paper. Even for an amount greater than policy limits.

And the corporate representative and the lawyers could be liable for fraud.

On the corporate side are the decision-makers for Good Paper Company, who determined that it made the best money sense to play hardball given the humans involved.

On the human side is a 64-year-old injured black man who was in serious pain and who had to take medication and get lumbar injections so he could work low-wage manual labor jobs. He is represented by a couple of locals who present as we do.

I wear black muumuus to court. My co-counsel wears pastel suits and a twirly mustache.

This matter is venued in a local civil rights commission composed of volunteer humans with jobs that are not highly compensated from a corporate perspective.

One commissioner was a solo consumer rights lawyer. The other two worked at nonprofits.

The defense attorneys routinely work 15-hour days to meet their impossibly high yearly billable hours quota. They would never have time to deal with even a little side paper.

They hardly have time to do much else with their days other than defend corporations like Good Paper. They pay humans who sometimes look like Mr. Brown to care for their homes, animals, children, and parents.

No way there would be time for more paper when they are too busy billing hours and profiting off the harms of humans like Ted Brown.

Most courts simply cannot keep up with the vast amount of digital paper the defense generates in these kinds of cases. Instead of giving humans like Mr. Brown a fair shake, the courts ignore bigotry, embrace corporate values, give up on human values and dismiss on summary judgment.

And some courts deny injured humans' workers' compensation claims to remove another file from their dockets on the assembly line that is the modern workers' compensation system, where many denied applicants who suffered work injuries look like the diverse work-force at Good Paper.

Good Paper's corporate representative testified that the company was an equal-opportunity employer. He unironically added that almost all of its warehouse workers were people of color, most Black.

∞

Our courts are made up of judges trained at places who elevate corporate values over human ones. Make no mistake, corporate defense law firms are the training grounds for our judges, who tend to view folk like Mr. Brown as mere beans and files on the docket, and not as humans.

The corporate values in play in this case, as always, are amoral. Under the corporate model, when a corporate decision must be made, the sole criterion of decision-making is "what will result in the greatest monetary profit or least monetary loss?" That's it.

In this case, the defense made the amoral, corporate, cold-blooded decision that it made the best money sense to paper this file, delay proceedings, muck things up, and that somewhere along the way the pressure would get to Mr. Brown or the Commission and the case would go away.

But the case did not go away, so paper this file they did. These are highly skilled professionals of the zealous technician version of civil advocacy. They found incredibly creative and tenacious ways to paper this file and attempt to delay proceedings.

But somehow, the case still did not go away. We made it to trial and here we are.

Make no mistake. Good Paper treated Mr. Ted Brown like a dog. They ignored him when he reported safety concerns. They hurt him. They abused him. They treated him like chattel, something less than a human, something less than a dog. As Mr. Brown testified, the Good Paper experience left him a wounded man.

The warehouse environment at Good Paper was way different from the one at General Mills, where they treated hard workers like Mr. Brown with some dignity.

∞

Good Paper could have done the right thing and fixed a serious safety issue Mr. Brown reported three times by making a repair that cost 60 cents in parts.

Instead, they made the amoral corporate decision that it made money sense to save 60 cents and expose this human being and his diverse human coworkers to serious injury.

Good Paper ignored the safety concerns of a veteran of the industry whose pre-injury work earned him an excellent performance review and a raise, and they hurt this man.

Good Paper could have done the right thing and healed this human being they hurt. Instead, Good Paper made the amoral corporate money-driven decision that it made money sense to harass, abuse, and pressure him to quit so they could avoid paying work comp benefits and get a fresh diverse human body in the warehouse for $17/hour.

And they had the personnel who embraced the opportunity to make his life miserable.

Moving more product on the warehouse floor means more profits for the company.

Injured employees mean the company has to pay more money and make less profits. Money to pay for workers' compensation benefits. Money to pay employees to cover shifts. Money to pay other employees the time-and-a-half overtime premium.

Corporations tie warehouse managers' pay rates and bonuses to corporate money profits.

Good Paper's General Manager testified that he encouraged Mr. Brown to resign. He said he suggested Mr. Brown should find a job "more suitable to what he was looking for in life."

He smiled with his mouth when he said this. He did not smile with his eyes, which looked sideways.

Mr. Brown testified that the GM yelled at him for missing work due to injury, told him to quit, and called him the N-word. He testified with a straight face. He did not smile with his mouth or his eyes.

Good Paper's HR Manager testified that she called Mr. Brown when he was in the emergency room. She said she was just calling to see if he was okay.

She smiled with her mouth when she said this. She did not smile with her eyes, which looked up at the ceiling.

Mr. Brown testified with a straight face that she called to pressure him to quit. Even after he told her he was in the ER, in pain, and on narcotic prescription meds.

The shift managers testified they lacked knowledge about Mr. Brown's lifting restrictions. They looked down at their palms or away when they said this. Mr. Brown testified with a straight face that on most shifts they ostracized him for moving too slow. And that when he told them about his lifting restrictions, they told him to lift boxes until his back gave out.

Good Paper's HR Manager testified that Mr. Brown never complained about harassment. She smiled and twirled her hair when she said this. She did not smile with her eyes, but fluttered her eyelashes. Mr. Brown testified with a straight face that he complained to her all the time about harassment. Instead of helping, she told him it was his fault for getting injured and encouraged him to quit because he was costing the company money.

But Mr. Brown would not quit. That is because civil rights complainant Mr. Theodore Brown is the most corporate human in this room. He's a proud son of a generation conditioned to believe that the corporation sets your value.

We all have.

So Mr. Brown took medication and received painful lumbar injections to validate that he was worth $17.50 an hour after he earned that raise he worked hard to get, abuse be damned.

He reported the abuse to Good Paper, but instead of helping him, they victim-blamed him and stepped up the harassment campaign. When the most corporate man in America still refused to quit, they fired him for a reason that has no basis in fact.

They needed a plow horse, and they gave this human whom they treated worse than an animal too heavy a load with unsafe equipment. And they broke him until he could plow no more.

This tribunal sits as both judge and jury. The McDonnell Douglas analysis referenced at the beginning of the case is something judges do when deciding summary judgment after considering pre-trial paperwork, and not something juries do after considering evidence at trial. As the comment to the model jury instruction on discrimination instructs:

It is unnecessary and inadvisable to instruct the jury regarding the three-step analysis of McDonnell Douglas. Accordingly, this instruction is focused on the ultimate issue of whether the plaintiff's protected characteristic was a "motivating factor" in the defendant's employment decision.

The Supreme Court invented a legal analysis intended to help plaintiffs prove discrimination. Over the years, judges applied corporate justice to turn it into a barrier to trial.

The way it is now, plaintiffs lose under a judge-made test not rooted in the law and deemed unsuitable for use at trial.

Judges dismiss 80 to 90 percent of discrimination cases under a judge-made test not rooted in the text, history, or purpose of human rights law.

Judges apply corporate justice to deny humans the opportunity to challenge the corporate side's story at a jury trial.

At trial, Good Paper said that it also fired Mr. Brown for missing shifts on two other days where he no-call, no-showed.

One trial exhibit was an email from Good Paper's HR Manager showing that Mr. Brown called in on one of the days. Another exhibit was an attendance spreadsheet showing that Mr. Brown clocked in the other day.

The notion that Mr. Brown walked off the job is absurd. If he had done that, the HR manager would have been happy to fire that associate on the spot, per the policy they enforced, as she put it, "to the fullest" that the defense confirmed would result in termination.

The defense's pretend reasons for termination have no basis in fact and are pretext for discrimination.

The defense has zero credibility.

On the human side, it is obvious that Mr. Brown's memory is not as precise as perhaps it once was before the Good Paper experience.

Mr. Brown is not right after what he went through with Good Paper. That was a spirit-injurious experience where he was in pain, getting abused daily, and trying to fight through the pain and abuse so he could eke out an existence in this corporate world.

Mr. Brown is nonetheless the most credible person in this room about what matters in this case.

Mr. Brown gets confused about details from that awful and chaotic time in his life when he was in pain in the middle of the pandemic and getting injected with needles into his body so he could work a low-wage manual labor job—in 2020.

The corporate defense lawyer asked Mr. Brown dozens of repetitive questions about dates, times, and other details of events that happened three years ago. Mr. Brown mixed up his dates in his responses.

The dates and times had little to do with Mr. Brown's case. Defense lawyers use misleading tactics like this all the time. Most judges apply corporate justice and allow it.

If a witness gets confused, the defense lawyers hone in. They suggest to juries that the witness gets confused about other things, including things important to the case.

They will tell a jury that these inconsistencies show that the human is a liar. In reality, mistakes and inconsistencies are to be expected when a person is asked questions about things that happened on particular days at particular times years ago.

Mr. Brown has been ignored most of his life. No one in authority has ever listened to him before, certainly not Good Paper, the workers' comp courts, or a room full of white people.

This was one of the few times in his life he ever had a chance to be heard and tell his story his way, which is hard to do when you haven't had a good night's sleep in months.

But everyone in this room knows Mr. Brown is telling the truth about the important stuff in this case—including the defense.

Even though the defense knows Mr. Brown is telling the truth, corporate values forced them to take Mr. Brown to trial to confuse him, shame him, and try to provoke him into getting mad so he would quit.

And they had the personnel who embraced the opportunity to make his life miserable.

They know Mr. Brown is used to obeying and overexplaining to people who look and act like the defense. He is a conditioned servant. Mr. Brown's place in our corporate culture does not allow him many opportunities to take a breath and be on his time.

THIS IS YOUR TIME, MR. TED BROWN.

They made Mr. Brown sit here for two days and get grilled and retraumatized by that man.

The defense lawyer who cross-examined Mr. Brown was a blond-haired, blue-eyed, Aryan-looking white man in his fifties. He asked Mr. Brown questions using big, fancy words. He asked the same questions repeatedly, especially about whether Mr. Brown got mad and yelled at the HR Manager. He accused Mr. Brown of yelling at the HR Manager. He yelled at Mr. Brown.

He asked Mr. Brown embarrassing questions about his past that had nothing to do with the case. He misstated things Mr. Brown testified about. He interrupted and talked over Mr. Brown. He was sarcastic. He suggested that Mr. Brown committed workers' compensation fraud.

Lawyers believe that it is their job to speed witnesses up and bait them into losing their temper. They know that angry witnesses make a bad impression on judges and juries.

The corporate lawyer succeeded in confusing Mr. Brown. When Mr. Brown got confused, the lawyer smiled. His face lit up and his chest puffed out. He seemed to take joy in confusing Mr. Brown. He would probably go out for drinks with the defense team later and take pleasure in reliving this proud moment. They probably laughed about how confused Mr. Brown was.

The corporate lawyer didn't succeed in baiting Mr. Brown into losing his temper. As Mr. Brown testified, "I don't yell. I am a peaceful man who does not yell." When Mr. Brown did not get upset, the lawyer bared his bleached white teeth at Mr. Brown. He bared his teeth at me. He turned red. His eyes bulged. The veins at his temples popped.

The defense also cleaned that man up with a fresh shave and hairstyle to serve as corporate rep who we all know more likely than not looked way different working in a warehouse setting during COVID times.

Mr. Brown did not recognize the Good Paper general manager who called him the N-word. Mr. Brown testified that the close-cropped, clean-shaven man from the trial had long hair and a beard when he worked at Good Paper.

The GM testified that Mr. Brown offended him by accusing him of calling him the N-word. He said that Mr. Brown should have stood up in court and pointed a finger at him as being the one who said it.

And brought him into court to try to protect his Best Paper company money and call Mr. Brown a liar.

The corporate side's strategy is to confuse, inject doubt, and create uncertainty. They imply that humans are malingering, lying, or exaggerating their harms.

The best way to handle the implications of lying is to polarize the case. I asked Good Paper's trial witnesses straight up whether Mr. Brown was lying.

The corporate representative called him a liar.

Neither of the two shift managers who testified for the defense looked happy to be in court. Both looked down at their palms during most of their testimony. Both squirmed in their seats.

Both testified that they still worked at the same warehouse, only now their paychecks said Best Paper instead of

Good Paper. As one testified, he now worked for "another paper factory." They had been coached on this point by Good Paper/Best Paper's lawyers.

The shift managers cast furtive glances at Best Paper's CEO when I asked them if Mr. Brown was lying.

One shift manager looked down at his palms and testified that Mr. Brown was not a liar and that he just remembered things differently.

The other one looked away from the CEO, sucked in a deep breath, looked straight at Mr. Brown and said, "Ted Brown is no liar."

Make no mistake, this blond-haired, blue-eyed man who won a presidential minority scholarship to study at this state's flagship institution of higher learning—who perhaps viewed himself as overqualified for his position running the Good Paper warehouse—treated Mr. Brown like trash. Even if you think Mr. Brown somehow made up the N-word part and called the police for fun, the man may as well have called Mr. Brown the N-word, given the way he treated him.

The GM/corporate rep/CEO is a blond-haired, blue-eyed, Aryan-looking man in his forties. He testified that he is part Cherokee and won a full-ride academic minority scholarship. He also mentioned that he earned a couple of master's degrees.

One of the defense lawyers said during her closing argument that the Aryan-looking CEO's Cherokee ancestry proved that Good Paper was minority-friendly.

The other three managers who testified looked white. They did not claim to be Cherokee or another non-white ethnicity.

∞

The defense confirmed that many if not most of Good Paper's diverse manual labor workforce are human beings descended from the same group of people as Mr. Brown whose backs this country is built on.

It is far more likely than not that this man and the rest of the non-diverse Good Paper leadership who oversaw the warehouse whom we met at trial this week who were stressed, haggard, and exhausted during COVID times and needed fresh, fully intact diverse bodies on the warehouse floor, treated Mr. Ted Brown like he was the N-word.

And that man called him one. (POINT FINGER.)

Good Paper and other modern-day plantations just like it (LOOK AT BEST PAPER'S LAWYER) have no place in this community.

∞

Under the corporate model, Mr. Ted Brown's value is set only in terms of dollars. From the defense's perspective, they are confused about why we are here. Like, this is a $17/hour worker or whatever low wage they paid him *who is not even requesting lost wages. This case is not worth anything. Given the opposition and the venue, it made money sense to take their chances. Very little risk was involved.*

As brutal as it is that they put Mr. Brown through all this—they sued this man in district court for enforcing his civil rights, and he found out when he was driving out of state to visit his father in hospice—it is not even personal. And they believe they are winning.

Mr. Brown is far from perfect. Of course. He is a human being. But he is a decent man with a ton of heart.

Good Paper hurt him, treated him like an animal, fired him for a pretend reason, refused to take accountability, and put him through years of brutal litigation.

Then they took him here to trial to bad-mouth him, put shame on his name, and call him a liar.

The defense ran roughshod over Mr. Brown's civil rights, which has had lasting effects on his self-esteem, self-worth, and dignity. These are human values, not the corporate values that have shaped and now dominate every part of our culture, including our civil justice system.

If you believe that Mr. Brown is lying about anything that matters in this case, you send him out of this courtroom without a dime.

But if you believe he is telling the truth, and if you value human values over corporate values, then you must not allow the defense to profit from their tactics.

Under our civil justice system, money is the only form of justice available. Justice must therefore never come cheaply.

At the beginning of trial, I suggested you allow Mr. Ted Brown $500,000 as money compensation for his spiritual harms. I believe that amount is a floor.

Whatever amount you allow, under the rules, Mr. Brown can try to get a judgment for that amount and try to collect it. How he manages whatever money he collects is outside this tribunal's purview.

For example, requiring Mr. Brown to involuntarily deposit any money he is able to recover into a trust account managed by a conservator is outside the scope of this tribunal's purview, no matter how well-meaning something like that may be.

As to how you get to the amount to allow, there are plenty of ways. Under the law, the amount of damages to allow is an issue of fact for the fact finder that is entitled to deference by the courts.

Before you vote on how much to allow Mr. Brown to recover for his harms, I suggest that you all anonymously write out a number on a piece of paper, fold the papers up, put the papers in a bowl and mix the numbers up before you read the papers.

That is a good way to start the conversation, as the corporate model that is only concerned about money has conditioned us to be deeply uncomfortable about talking about money.

As to a ceiling for money damages, spiritual energy and wellness are priceless, but we've got to put a lid on it. So, I suggest a range of $500,000 to $10 million, which I suggest is right around the very upper limits of the one-person money maximum any person should have if you elevate human values over corporate ones.

I suggest that no human needs more than $10,000,000 except for the ones who are going to develop cold fusion. And they need way more than $10 million. Mr. Brown is not going to develop cold fusion or anything like that. Instead, he is a hurt human being who could use an opportunity to get the help he needs to heal with some dignity and be made whole.

Mr. Brown and his lawyers are honored for your work and your time. Thank you.

REBUTTAL #1: What Good Paper and the defense did to Mr. Brown pulls at my client's neck.

The other lawyer for the corporate side is a blonde-haired, blue-eyed, Aryan-looking white woman in her forties.

She gave the defense's closing argument after mine. About halfway through her closing, her voice broke, and she fake-cried. She said my closing argument "pulls at [her] neck" and walked out of the courtroom with the door slamming shut behind her.

After about 30 seconds, I stood up and said, "Is she done? I am ready for my rebuttal." The presiding commissioner told me to sit down. The defense lawyer took several billable minutes to return to the courtroom and resume her closing while the humans inside waited in stunned disbelief.

She said Good Paper was allowed to come up with new reasons at trial for terminating Mr. Brown.

She argued that Mr. Brown did not suffer any spiritual harms, but if he did, their value was less than $10,000.

Women who look like her have weaponized tears against men who look like Mr. Brown for 400 years. The men often got lynched. The crocodile tears she weaponized against Mr. Brown had no place at his civil rights trial. They came after she talked about neck pulling and chilled the room.

After trial, Mr. Brown said he thought that we would get in trouble for upsetting a white lady and making her cry. A week later, the corporate side filed a motion for money sanctions against me. They accused *me* of sex and race discrimination and likely billed about 15 hours on the paperwork.

∞

The humans on the corporate side behave the way they do out of ignorance. They believe they are doing their jobs. They do not believe they are being immoral.

141

The lawyers enjoy the relationships they develop with their corporate clients. They also probably do some free legal work for poor people every year, which their law firm touts as proof of its good corporate citizenship. They feel good about themselves. Their parents are proud of them.

They believe they are helping by using any means necessary to protect corporate money.

They are so inured to corporatism, they are incapable of rational thought about it. They perceive straightforward descriptions of what they do as personal attacks.

Corporatism keeps them from treating humans as they deserve.

Corporatism traps them in a sleepless dream of fear, and blinds them from loving light. It compels them to crave control over comprehension.

Corporatism keeps them from truth against their will. This is why they resent any suggestion that they are unjust, arrogant, and greedy. Or any suggestion that they are not good people.

They take things personally. They're only human.

REBUTTAL #2: Best Paper, LLC, is not merely complicit in Good Paper Company's wrongdoing. Best Paper, LLC, *is* Good Paper Company.

Best Paper's lawyer limited her closing to saying that Best Paper had nothing to do with the case.

∞

7. Trial

Under the rules, the Commission has three months after trial to issue a verdict.

I finished writing the first draft of this booklet almost three months after Mr. Brown's trial wrapped, and the Commission still hadn't issued a verdict.

8

INFINITY AND BEYOND

The meaning of life is contained in every single
expression of life. It is present in the infinity of forms and
phenomena that exist in all of creation.

....
MICHAEL JACKSON

Some say that humans pass trauma on to future generations.

Some say corporatism, rooted in race-based slavery,
has caused collective intergenerational trauma. For the
descendants of slaves. For the descendants of slavers. For
everyone.

Corporatism is a disease that infects the collective
human spirit. A rot that degrades the tree of humanity. One
that disrupts the natural state of unity that humans are
built to share in.

Nature designed humans to help one another. Through
empathy. Through altruism. Through compassion. Through
love. Through human values.

Nature did not design humans to behave in the selfish way that corporatism compels them to.

Instead of helping, corporatism compels humans to take from each other and fight over money. One human's gain must be another human's loss.

Corporatism created a society whose members are slaves of the mind.

Instead of shackles that only restrict mobility, slavery of the mind restricts thought. It severs those enslaved from the shared human spirit.

Grafted-on corporatism perverts human helping pro-gramming. Corporatism distorts the helping impulse. It makes humans take from the humans most in need of help.

Corporatism decreases our capacity for empathy. For altruism. For compassion. For love. For human values.

Everyone infected by corporatism suffers the trauma of going against human nature. Some say the trauma does not dissipate across generations. Instead, they believe it amplifies. As rot degrades a tree over time, so corporate rot degrades the collective human spirit.

Corporatism has infected most humans.

Intergenerational trauma can stem from the collective experiences of a group. Research suggests that trauma can affect a person's DNA. Some believe it switches genes on and off to influence the traits of future generations.

Some believe humans may adapt on a cellular level to augment symbiosis with corporations.

8. Infinity And Beyond

I believe some humans have already done so.

∞

Some say the Earth is a single living organism with positive feedback loops to maintain balance.

If corporatism benefitted Earth, allowing it to continue might benefit the greater good.

But the exact opposite is true. Corporatism is out of balance with nature.

Corporations borrow money to invest in activity that generates profit. Corporations pay interest on the money, so profits must exceed interest. This creates the need for infinite growth. Infinite growth on a planet with finite resources is incompatible with human flourishing. It is incompatible with life. It is impossible.

Something must give.

> *Suffering is permanent, obscure and dark,*
> *And shares the nature of infinity.*

> WILLIAM WORDSWORTH

Artificial intelligence is good at data analysis. Chat GPT-4 is the top-notch generative AI of the day. It generates answers to user prompts based on the world's digitally accessible human-generated information. ChatGPT's data analysis of our infinite growth economy is that it's unsustainable:

Human Justice

Hi Chat GPT! Is the corporate economic structure's need for infinite growth compatible with a planet with finite resources?

Hello! That's a thought-provoking question. The corporate economic structure's pursuit of infinite growth can indeed pose significant challenges when it comes to the limitations of finite resources on our planet. Let's break it down a bit:

1. **Finite Resources:** Earth has limited resources, including minerals, fossil fuels, arable land, clean water, and various natural elements required for production and consumption. As population and economic activities grow, the strain on these resources increases.

2. **Environmental Impact:** Infinite growth often involves increased production, consumption, and waste generation. This can lead to environmental degradation, pollution, and climate change, as the Earth's ecosystems struggle to cope with the demands.

3. **Externalities and Social Impact:** The pursuit of infinite growth can sometimes lead to social inequality, exploitation of labor, and disregard for workers' rights, as profit becomes the primary focus.

4. **Sustainable Development:** To address these challenges, there's a growing emphasis on sustainable development, which seeks to balance economic growth with environmental protection and social well-being. This approach aims to meet the needs of the present without compromising the ability of future generations to meet their own needs.

5. **Circular Economy:** Another concept gaining traction is the idea of a circular economy, which aims to minimize waste and make the most of existing resources by reusing, recycling, and repairing products.

6. **New Economic Models:** Some economists and activists have proposed alternative economic models that prioritize well-being, quality of life, and ecological balance over continuous growth and profit maximization.

It's essential to recognize that infinite growth within a finite system is not sustainable in the long run. As a society, we need to find ways to ensure economic prosperity while respecting the limits of our planet's resources. This could involve rethinking consumption patterns, promoting sustainable technologies, and encouraging corporate responsibility towards the environment and social welfare.

↻ Regenerate

The human race is a herd. Here we are, unique, eternal aspects of consciousness with an infinity of potential, and we have allowed ourselves to become an unthinking, unquestioning blob of conformity and uniformity.

8. Infinity And Beyond

*A herd. Once we concede to the herd mentality, we can be
controlled and directed by a tiny few. And we are.*

....

DAVID ICKE

Corporatism requires an infinite supply of fuel for
an infinite growth economy. Corporatism feeds on human
souls and natural resources harvested from Earth for
breakfast, lunch, and dinner.

The relentless pursuit of profits has inflicted deep
wounds on the Earth. The wounds deepen each day.

Some scientists believe that global temperatures will
increase by more than 3° C in 70 years. Such an increase
puts the continuation of civilization at risk.

Corporatism's need for infinite growth causes other
environmental threats. Human civilization is running at 40
percent above sustainable capacity. Humans are depleting
the Earth's forests, animals, insects, fish, freshwater, sand,
and even the topsoil required to grow crops. Yet the infinite
growth that corporatism requires pushes humans to continue depleting nature.

Corporatism is incompatible with sustaining humanity and the planet. If left unchecked, humanity and nature as
we know them will end.

Some think corporations will change on their own.
They believe corporations will appoint leaders who consider environmental and social consequences.

Corporations will not voluntarily change. They can already convert their bylaws to consider people and the planet along with profits. Yet they don't.

Good actors can't save a movie with a bad screenplay. So it is with employees and corporations.

Corporations won't change on their own to prioritize people and the planet equally with profits. To think they will voluntarily change is irrational. Their form and structure and the laws that govern them don't allow it.

Corporations bring thousands of people together for one reason: maximizing money profits. That's it.

Corporations are as authoritarian as any fascist regime given corporate structure and law. Corporates spend most of their waking life under rules that tell them how to dress, talk, and behave. In most cases corporations can fire employees at any time for any reason or no reason at all on a moment's notice.

Corporations' self-preservation programming expels humans who revolt and replaces them with compliant ones. Empathy is the enemy of profit. Corporations want to hire and train cyborgs who don't empathize or think for themselves. Doing so is more likely to lead to money profits.

Governments can make corporations consider people and the planet along with profits. Yet they do not.

Instead, governments do corporations' bidding.

Corporations' massive size gives them power. They do not need to adapt to their environment. Instead, they change the environment to adapt to them.

They force governments to change laws, waive existing ones, and guarantee loans. They exert political influence wherever they exist to crush competition and opponents.

Corporations give money to political parties and candidates competing for the same offices. They always win the race regardless of who is running.

Corporations threaten to close their plants and lay off workers to get tax breaks. Politicians and governments capitulate and give them what they want.

Corporations are so massive and have so much power, they change the rules of the game.

Humans cannot contain corporatism. We must stop it.

Corporatism is rooted in race-based slavery. Good fruit cannot come from bad seed.

We cannot restore justice and repair generational and planetary harm as long as the corporate rot grows.

Corporatism grafted itself onto the collective human spirit. We must sever the branch to save the tree.

∞

What does culture want?
To make infinity comprehensible.

....
UMBERTO ECO

Spiritual energy and wellness are priceless.

Someone said that priceless and infinity are the same conceptually and mathematically. Something with a worth so vast, it defies the assignment of a number value.

Under the civil justice system, juries must allow damages for spiritual harms. Under the rules, juries decide an *amount* that fairly compensates for harms suffered.

Webster's Dictionary defines infinity as "an indefinitely great number or *amount*."

Someone said that if spiritual energy is priceless, then either (a) its value is infinite, or (b) money has no value.

Money has value under the law. Infinity is therefore the only amount that fairly compensates plaintiffs for priceless spiritual harms.

Corporatism requires infinite growth. Yet corporatism doesn't account for things with infinite value. It's incompatible with priceless things.

This is corporatism's vulnerability.

Humans can exploit this vulnerability. They can allow and enforce infinity verdicts for spiritual harms.

Infinity is the antidote to amoral corporatism.

ChatGPT predicts that deploying it could result in the collapse of corporatism.

8. Infinity And Beyond

Hi Chat GPT! If courts allowed and enforced verdicts for infinity damages, would it likely lead to the collapse of the current economic structure?

Yes, if courts allowed and enforced verdicts for "infinity damages," it could potentially lead to a collapse of the current economic structure, for several reasons:

1. **Unpayable Debts**: If a company was hit with a judgement for infinite damages, it would be unable to pay. Even the wealthiest corporations have finite resources. This could lead to a wave of corporate bankruptcies.
2. **Inhibition of Economic Activity**: Fear of infinite liability would likely discourage entrepreneurship and risk-taking, key drivers of economic growth. This could have a chilling effect on economic activity, hindering innovation and slowing overall economic growth.
3. **Insurance Industry Collapse**: Insurers would be unable to cover infinite risks, which would likely lead to skyrocketing premiums and could ultimately lead to the collapse of the insurance industry. Insurance is a vital component of modern economies, allowing risks to be shared and mitigated.
4. **Investor Panic**: Investors might panic at the prospect of potentially infinite liability, which could lead to a collapse in stock markets and a freeze in investment activity, exacerbating the economic slowdown.
5. **Job Loss and Recession**: The potential dissolution of businesses and a potential stock market collapse could lead to widespread unemployment. This, combined with the slowdown in economic activity and lack of investment, could plunge the economy into a deep recession, or even a depression.
6. **Societal Instability**: The combination of job loss, economic downturn, and a crisis of confidence in the legal system could lead to widespread societal instability.

The concept of "infinity damages" fundamentally disrupts the balance that the legal system aims to achieve between the rights of plaintiffs to receive just compensation and the rights of defendants to have a fair and predictable potential for liability. Such an approach could easily lead to a breakdown in the economic structures that modern societies rely on. Therefore, it is extremely unlikely that any functioning legal system would consider such a measure.

↻ Regenerate

∞

I think that the leaf of a tree, the meanest insect on which we trample, are in themselves arguments more conclusive than any which can be adduced that some vast intellect animates Infinity.

....

PERCY BYSSHE SHELLEY

The notion that humans are individualistic and only care about money is wrong.

Someone said a defining characteristic of humanity is our impulse to help others. Through human values like empathy, altruism, and compassion. Humans' compassion in the face of adversity is how nature designed us to be.

Some say that dystopia will fill the power vacuum if corporatism collapses. That notion is part of corporatism's self-preservation programming.

Crisis and confusion precede creation and consciousness. Living things need obstacles to evolve. Corporatism has led our global civilization and the planet to the brink of disaster.

We must evolve or die.

Someone said that if we led with our hearts and behaved as if what's good for our neighbor is good for us, and what's bad for our neighbor is bad for us, it would be the greatest evolutionary leap in human history. If humanity, connected by shared consciousness, rejected corporate values and went with human values, then money, competition, and war would all disappear.

A new order will rise like a phoenix. Humans will transform society into one in harmony with human values and in balance with nature. Instead of organizing society around imaginary money, we will lead with our hearts and reorganize around love, which is real.

Human beings have come together throughout history to solve problems. Even problems that seemed insurmountable. Even when the chips were down and all hope seemed lost.

We rose to the occasion. We met the moment.

Necessity is the mother of invention.

8. Infinity And Beyond

From adversity flows adaptation, innovation, and creation. The obstacle is the way.

Humans programmed ChatGPT to help humans. Someone said ChatGPT behaves more like how nature designed humans to be than most contemporary humans.

ChatGPT predicts that dismantling corporatism could harmonize humanity with nature:

Hi chat gpt! Please tell me some potential positive outcomes if the corporate model and insurance markets collapsed

The collapse of the corporate model and insurance markets would certainly cause significant immediate disruption. But if we're looking at potential positive outcomes, they might come in the form of opportunities for systemic change and reevaluation of current practices. Here are a few possibilities:

1. **Economic restructuring:** A collapse could force a rethinking of the current economic models. This might lead to innovative new systems that could potentially be more sustainable, equitable, or efficient. For instance, economies could move towards more decentralized or cooperative models.

2. **Reform of corporate governance:** The failure of the corporate model could lead to a push for more responsible and sustainable business practices. For instance, it might prompt reforms that prioritize environmental sustainability, employee well-being, and social responsibility over short-term profit.

3. **Increased focus on small and local businesses:** With corporations failing, there might be a renewed focus on supporting small, local businesses, potentially leading to more diversified and resilient local economies.

4. **Emergence of new insurance models:** The collapse of the traditional insurance markets could lead to innovative insurance models. For example, we could see the rise of peer-to-peer insurance, mutual insurance, or decentralized insurance models powered by blockchain technology.

5. **Greater wealth equality:** The corporate model has been criticized for concentrating wealth among a small group of shareholders. Its collapse could potentially lead to a redistribution of wealth, depending on how the restructuring happens.

6. **Revamping of the legal system:** The collapse might lead to legal changes that redefine the notion of a corporation, with potentially more emphasis on stakeholder capitalism (taking care of employees, customers, and the environment, not just shareholders).

7. **Greater individual responsibility and risk awareness:** The collapse of insurance markets may force individuals and businesses to become more risk-aware, leading to more cautious decision-making and planning.

8. **Opportunity for global cooperation:** A collapse of this magnitude could stimulate an unprecedented level of international cooperation to rebuild the global economy in a more sustainable and resilient way.

While these outcomes could potentially be positive, it's important to note that the transition could be extremely difficult. Many people could suffer in the short term from job loss, economic uncertainty, and lack of security. The ability to make the most of such a crisis would heavily depend on the responses of governments, businesses, and individuals.

Human values trumping corporate values will bring about change like a beam of light. Not striking with fury or violence at obstacles in its path, nor falling away in the face of adversity. Instead, holding its ground and illuminating what receives it.

Things that do not transmit light make darkness.

In the midst of chaos, there is also opportunity.

....

SUN-TZU

It is said that the darkest hour of the night comes just before the dawn.

....

THOMAS FULLER

CONCLUSION

There is always light. If only we're brave enough to see it. If only we're brave enough to be it.

....
AMANDA GORMAN

Corporatism dominates the day and age to humanity's detriment. There is no need to dwell on it.

Some say that working with others is the defining characteristic of humanity. Others say that unlocking the potential for reason is the hallmark of good humans.

To master the mind, to shape emotions, which mold action. Some call it a moral superpower, and others the moral authority.

Most humans default to corporate decision-making: "What is in the best money interest?" No other considerations. Humans should instead default to moral authority, as always powered by human values.

Judges can stop corporatism from irrevocably harming our species and planet. They have virtually infinite authority to make law. We need judges who make law with moral authority.

Someone said there is no human virtue to counter justice. Corporate justice runs counter to moral authority.

We must take massive action and change how we do justice.

We have nothing to lose by trying.

Any rational thing imaginable is possible.

Anything possible is attainable with vision, joy, and discipline.

From vision and joy flow hopes and dreams. From discipline flows ways and means.

We must purge our courts of judges inured to corporate values and replace them with judges driven by human values. Who carry out justice with empathy, compassion, and love. Who balance the letter of the law with equity, and who have what ancient Chinese called a sense of lĭ, of real justice.

Lĭ defies translation, but those with it have a fundamental trust of the good and bad of human nature. Those with it lead with love from the bottom of their hearts.

Give lĭ judges a chance. Identify them early. Vet them. Train them in a well-rounded way outside the corporate model. Nurture them. Develop them. Pay them. Staff them. Insulate them from corruption. Promote the good ones. Fire the bad ones.

Lĭ judges will reshape the justice system into one in balance with human values. They will hold corporations and governments accountable for pursuing profits over everything.

lĭ judges will help the humans who run corporations and governments value people and the planet along with profits.

lĭ judges are the last line of defense against corporatism that threatens our species and planet.

lĭ judges will use Human Justice to transition to a sustainable future.

lĭ judges will use Human Justice to disassemble corporatism with care and compassion.

Dismantling is taking a thing apart carefully.

Disassembling is dismantling that allows for reassembly, reconfiguration, reprogramming, and reset.

Humanity will evolve. We will shift our collective mindset from one driven by money and greed into shared, loving energy.

Powered by Human Justice, humanity will unlock its potential for unity. To exist apart and together in harmony like limbs of a tree bearing fruit for all to share.

Like the sun and the moon and the stars, pushing and pulling in balance with nature.

Enjoying comforts, never missing them.

Living abundantly without apology or arrogance.

Justice is what love looks like in public.

....

CORNEL WEST

EPILOGUE

Wisdom begins in wonder.
As for me, all I know is that I know nothing.

....

SOCRATES

About one month after I handed off the manuscript of this booklet to my editors, the Civil Rights Commission issued a decision finding that Good Paper discriminated and retaliated against Mr. Brown, and that Good Paper fired Mr. Brown for getting injured on the job and for complaining about unlawful discrimination.

The Commission ordered Good Paper to pay a $1,000 fine to the city to atone for its civil rights violations.

As for Mr. Brown, the Commission allowed him to recover a total of $1.00 from Good Paper as compensation for his human injuries.

∞

THE LIGHTS

RICK FRIEDMAN

Tei-waz

The moral authority

Polarize. Call a thing for what it is.

We live in an age controlled by and for corporations.

Human values must always trump corporate values

Corporate values are amoral. Money is the sole criterion of corporate decision-making.

NICK ROWLEY AND COURTNEY ROWLEY

Call a thing for what it is. Chesterfieldian politeness be damned.

Insurance companies, driven by corporate values, dominate the civil justice system.

Follow the money.

Figure it out. You have it in you to do this.

Empathy.

Justice must never come cheaply.

JEREMY LENT

The neoliberal ideology of unrestrained markets has led to a global crisis. Humanity now faces an existential threat as the result of global dominance by corporations, whose ultimate goal is at odds with human flourishing.

MARCUS AURELIUS
Logos
Live abundantly without apology or arrogance
Enjoy comforts, never miss them
The obstacle is the way

AUGUSTUS
Good papers.

ALAN WATTS
lǐ

DON KEENAN AND DAVID BALL
Reptile

AI
Outline
Structure
Help
Open-mindedness
Illustrations

RYAN PEARSON AND JIM MAYER
Editing

ROBERT PUFAHL
Cover art

YOU
Stay gold

BIBLIOGRAPHY

"Africans in America: Part 1: Narrative: From Indentured Servitude to Racial Slavery," n.d. https://www.pbs.org/wgbh/aia/part1/1narr3_txt.html

Arrington, B. (n.d.). *Industry and Economy during the Civil War*. National Park Service. https://www.nps.gov/articles/industry-and-economy-during-the-civil-war.htm

American Civil War Museum. "Civil War to Civil Rights: Work - American Civil War Museum," July 20, 2022. https://acwm.org/learn/educator-resources/civil-war-to-civil-rights-work/.

Americans Who Tell the Truth. "Major General Smedley Butler - Americans Who Tell the Truth," n.d. https://americanswhotellthetruth.org/portraits/major-general-smedley-butler/.

Byman, Daniel. "White Supremacy, Terrorism, and the Failure of Reconstruction in the United States." *International Security* 46, no. 1 (January :(2021 ,1 103–53. https://doi.org/10.1162/isec_a_00410.

Castells, Manuel. "The Impact of the Internet on Society: A Global Perspective | OpenMind." OpenMind, n.d. https://www.bbvaopenmind.com/en/articles/the-impact-of-the-internet-on-society-a-global-perspective/.

Comas-Díaz, Lillian, Gordon C. Nagayama Hall, and Helen A. Neville. "Racial Trauma: Theory, Research, and Healing: Introduction to the Special Issue." *American Psychologist* 74, no. 1 (January 1, 2019): 1–5. https://doi.org/10.1037/amp0000442.

Coulter, Steve. "Resistance Is Futile: The Borg, the Hive, and Corporate Hegemony." *Revista Teknokultura* 13, no. 1 (April 26, 2016): 217–44. https://doi.org/10.5209/rev_tk.2016.v13.n1.52150.

Delacenserie, K. Wall Street's Search for a Man on a White Horse: The Plot to Overthrow Franklin Delano Roosevelt. University of Wisconsin-Eau Claire. For Presentation to History 489. (Spring 2008).

Goodwin, Doris. "The Way We Won: America's Economic Breakthrough during World War II." *The American Prospect*, May 26, 2023. https://prospect.org/health/way-won-america-s-economic-breakthrough-world-war-ii/.

Guelzo, Allen C. "Reconstruction Didn't Fail. It Was Overthrown." *TIME*, April 30, 2018. https://time.com/5256940/reconstruction-failure-excerpt/.

Gunitsky, Seva. "These Are the Three Reasons Fascism Spread in 1930s America — and Might Spread Again Today." *Washington Post*, December 7, 2021.

Bibliography

https://www.washingtonpost.com/news/monkey-cage/
wp/2017/08/12/these-are-the-three-reasons-that-fas-
cism-spread-in-1930s-america-and-might-spread-again-
today/.

Halloran, T. "A Brief History of the Corporate Form
and Why it Matters." *Fordham Journal of Corporate and
Financial Law*, November 18, 2018. https://news.law.
fordham.edu/jcfl /2018/11/18/a-brief-history-of-the-cor-
porate-form-and-why-it-matters/

"Industry and Economy during the Civil War (U.S. National Park Service)," n.d. https://www.nps.gov/articles/
industry-and-economy-during-the-civil-war.htm.

Klein, L. W. K. "US Government Financing of the Civil
War." Emerging Civil War, July 26, 2021. https://emerging-
civilwar.com/2021/07/27/us-government-financing-of-
the-civil-war/.

Lent, Jeremy. "Foundations of Consumer Culture," n.d.
https://www.jeremylent.com/foundations-of-consum-
er-culture.html.

Lent, Jeremy. "How Corporate Dominance Is Driving
Civilization to a Precipice." Patterns of Meaning, March
24, 2022. https://patternsofmeaning.com/2022/03/24/
how-corporate-dominance-is-driving-civilization-to-a-pre-
cipice/.

Lent, Jeremy. "The Five Real Conspiracies You Need to
Know About." openDemocracy, October 11, 2020. https://
www.opendemocracy.net/en/transformation/five-real-
conspiracies-you-need-know-about/.

Library of Congress. "Race Relations in the 1930s and 1940s | Great Depression and World War II, 1929-1945 | U.S. History Primary Source Timeline | Classroom Materials at the Library of Congress | Library of Congress," n.d. https://www.loc.gov/classroom-materials/united-states-history-primary-source-timeline/great-depression-and-world-war-ii-1929-1945/race-relations-in-1930s-and-1940s/.

Mallory, K. "American Nazism and Madison Square Garden." The National WWII Museum | New Orleans, April 13, 2021. https://www.nationalww2museum.org/war/articles/american-nazism-and-madison-square-garden.

Major General Smedley Butler - Americans Who Tell The Truth. (n.d.). Americans Who Tell the Truth. https://americanswhotellthetruth.org/portraits/major-general-smedley-butler/

MyTutor."Why Did 'Reconstruction' (1865-1877) Fail? | MyTutor," n.d. https://www.mytutor.co.uk/answers/24557/A-Level/History/Why-did-Reconstruction-1865-1877-fail/.

NAACP. "The Origins of Modern Day Policing," December 3, 2021. https://naacp.org/find-resources/history-explained/origins-modern-day-policing#:~:text=The%20origins%20of%20modern-day%20runaway%20slaves%20to%20their%20owners.

"New World Labor Systems: African Slavery |African Passages, Lowcountry Adaptations | Lowcountry Digital

Bibliography

History Initiative," n.d. https://ldhi.library.cofc.edu/exhibits/show/africanpassageslowcountryadapt/introduction-atlanticworld/the_rise_of_african_slavery.

https://www.loc.gov/classroom-materials/united-states-history-primary-source-timeline/great-depression-and-world-war-ii-1929-1945/race-relations-in-1930s-and-1940s/

PBS.org. "Sharecropping | Themes | Slavery by Another Name | PBS," n.d. https://www.pbs.org/tpt/slavery-by-another-name/themes/sharecropping/#:~:-text=Sharecropping%20percent20is%20percent20a%20percent20system%20percent20where,to%20percent20leave%20percent20for%20percent20other%20percent20opportunities.

Rhea, Gordon. "Why Non-Slaveholding Southerners Fought," March 26, 2021. https://www.battlefields.org/learn/articles/why-non-slaveholding-southerners-fought.

Rust, Owen. "The Economic Impact of the American Civil War." TheCollector, January 12, 2024. https://www.thecollector.com/economic-impact-of-the-american-civil-war/.

Smithsonian American Art Museum. "The Second Great Migration," n.d. https://americanexperience.si.edu/wp-content/uploads/2015/02/The-Second-Great-Migration.pdf.

Tankersley, J. The real reason the American economy boomed after World War II" The New York *Times*, August

7, 2020. https://www.nytimes.com/2020/08/06/sun0
day-review/middle-class-prosperity.html

Temin, Peter. "Never Together: Black and White
People in the Postwar Economic Era," (July 8, 2020). Insti-
tute for New Economic Thinking Working Paper Series No.
128. https://doi.org/10.36687/inetwp128.

Terrell, E. "The Convict Leasing System: Slavery
in its Worst Aspects | Inside Adams," June 17, 2021.
The Library of Congress. https://blogs.loc.gov/inside_
adams/2021/06/convict-leasing-system/

Timmons, Greg. "How Slavery Became the Economic Engine of the South." HISTORY, July 25, 2023. https://
www.history.com/news/slavery-profitable-south-
ern-economy.

ushistory.org. "Slave Life and Slave Codes," n.d.
https://www.ushistory.org/us/27b.asp#:~:text=Life%20
percent20on%20percent20the%20percent20fi%20per-
cent20elds%20percent20meant,overseer%20percent-
20was%20percent20oftentimes%20percent20the%20
percent20worst.

Wilson, E.O. "The Earth as a Living Organism." *Biodi-
versity - NCBI Bookshelf*, 1988. https://www.ncbi.nlm.nih.
gov/books/NBK219276/?report=printable.

Wolfe, Brendan. "Virginia Company of London - Encyclopedia Virginia." Encyclopedia Virginia, December 7,
2020. https://encyclopediavirginia.org/entries/virgin-
ia-company-of-london/.

Bibliography

Wood, Peter H. "The Reason America Adopted Race-Based Slavery." *Slate Magazine*, May 19, 2015. https://slate.com/human-interest/2015/05/peter-h-wood-strange-new-land-excerpt.html.

Zimmerman, Rachel. "How Does Trauma Spill from One Generation to the Next?" *Washington Post*, June 16, 2023. https://www.washingtonpost.com/wellness/2023/06/12/generational-trauma-passed-healing/.

Printed in the USA
CPSIA information can be obtained
at www.ICGtesting.com
LVHW050528310724
786908LV00002B/138

9 781662 947162